Operations Research
for Public Systems

Operations Research for Public Systems

PHILIP M. MORSE, *Editor*

assisted by
LAURA W. BACON

 The M.I.T. Press
Massachusetts Institute of Technology
Cambridge, Massachusetts, and London, England

PREFACE

During the past five years an increasing number of experts have become persuaded that the procedures of operations research would be effective in solving some of the problems of the public sector, such as those in urban operations, in public health, and in education, for example. Operations research professionals, noting the success of applications in the industrial and the military sectors, became convinced that many of their methods, such as system modeling, computer simulation, mathematical programming, and the application of the theory of stochastic processes, could be useful in public affairs -- indeed, that the public sector urgently needed this kind of assistance. At the same time a growing number of managers of public operations and experts in urban and regional planning became aware of operations research and began to be interested in trying out its techniques. Thus a present need is to establish communication between the two groups, to indicate to the operations research expert the nature of some of the problems in the public sector which might be amenable to present operations research procedures and to describe to managers and planners of public systems the ways in which operations research could assist them.

Obviously the description of a few case histories of actual application would expedite this intercommunication; such examples would enable the discussion to advance beyond vague generalities and would point up the difficulties as well as the potentialities. Not until the past year was it considered possible to assemble a wide enough variety of such case histories to make feasible a planned colloquy between managers and planners of public systems and operations research professionals. A Special Summer Program on "Operations Research in Public Affairs" was held at M.I.T. from September 6 through September 10, 1966; it was attended by 20 experts from the public sector and 20 operations research specialists with experience in public systems applications. This volume is the result of that Program.

Nearly all the work reported in the Program was in process; most of the findings were preliminary and, of course, the coverage of the field was quite incomplete. For example, a significant number of important European studies were not included. Usual practice would have delayed publication of the reported material for several years, by which time final results could be included and the relative success of the various studies could be evaluated. The participants in the Program, however, felt that there were persuasive reasons for speeding up this process, in order to further intercommunication.

Thus, although the material reported in this volume is not in final or scholarly form, it is hoped that it will help the managers and planners of public systems to understand what operations research can do -- and cannot do -- for them and that it will arouse the interest of more operations analysts in problems in the public sector. If this dual goal is achieved, the contributors to this volume will consider their venture successful; if it contributes toward improving the efficiency and feasibility of public systems, it will have been worth the effort.

In addition to the authors of the various Chapters, many others contributed time and thought to the Program and to the present book. The 40-odd participants in the Program contributed through their lively discussion of each presentation. The Messrs. Earl D. Brown, Terrence E. Daniel, Avinash Dixit, Robert J. Gladstone, Hans A. Herriger, John B. Jennings, Ralph L. Keeney, Dev K. Ray, and Dr. Carl A. Zehnder, associates and graduate assistants of the M.I.T. Operations Research Center, were very helpful in reporting the discussions and in assisting several authors to put their Chapters into final form.

Cambridge, Massachusetts   Philip M. Morse
May, 1967   Laura W. Bacon

CONTENTS

Chapter 1

INTRODUCTION

Philip M. Morse

1.1 Operations Research in Action

The papers presented at the Summer Program in Operations Research, which are the basis for the Chapters of this volume, are concerned with applications in the area of public affairs of a branch of applied science which has been successfully applied to many other areas of human activity. This applied science is variously called operations research or management science or systems analysis. It proceeds by analyzing the quantitative aspects of the human activity, the operation; by developing mathematical models which represent some of the inter-relations between these aspects; and by using the model to predict the reaction of the operation to various possible changes in external or internal influences. These predictions are then available to the manager of the operation, to assist him in choosing between alternative policies and plans.

Examples of Industrial and Military Applications. Operations research was first applied to military problems,[7] where it was so successful in working out the inter-relations between one's own tactics and those of the enemy, that most armed forces now have operations research teams reporting to their top staffs and carrying on continuing analysis of military plans and operation. Early success during World War II was in part due to the great pressures and rapid changes of circumstance then occurring. These gave a great advantage to the ability to analyze rapidly the effect of changes and to predict the resulting shifts of pressure. Tactical and, eventually, strategic decisions could be made more quickly and with greater insight into the consequences.

In the past twenty years operations research has been applied with increasing success to industrial and commercial operations. The successes at first were in the relatively simple portions of the operation, such things as the behavior of inventory in the face of the variability of supply and demand, and the scheduling of production in such a way as to utilize most effectively the machinery on hand. These elements could most easily be represented by mathematical models, and the

1

implications of changes in inventory or production policy could
be predicted with fair accuracy. Many companies have saved
substantial sums of money by applying operations research to
these parts of their operations.[1] Certainly the simple aspects
of school operation, such as inventory control and class scheduling, could be improved by employing the same methods.

With increased knowledge of the workings of the simpler
elements and with the resulting increased cooperation and
trust of industrial management in their operations research
staffs, broader problems of system integration and long-range
planning are now being solved. The location of new factories
and warehouses are worked out to minimize transport costs
and to maximize accessibility to markets. Data on the elements
of the operation are often kept in accessible form on computers
so that the implications of various production or marketing
plans can be worked out quickly, to assist management in
deciding between alternative policies under consideration.

Using the O. R. Team. In solving the simpler problems,
where more exact mathematical models are possible, persons
with backgrounds in mathematics and physical science have
usually been most effective. With systems of greater complexity, the exactness of the model is less likely of achievement,
and experts in other disciplines become more useful as members
of the operations research team. Persons with backgrounds in
economics, psychology, and other social sciences have expertise
which can greatly assist in the analysis. Indeed, one characteristic of the teams which have been most successful in solving
these complex problems has been their interdisciplinary makeup.
The outstanding results in the field of military planning by the
RAND Corporation[11] and in the fields of industrial and urban
planning by the consulting firm of A. D. Little are examples of
the power of mixed teams of exact and social scientists in
analyzing these highly complex administrative problems.

It should be emphasized that the procedures of operations
research are not expected to provide all the bases for managerial
decisions; the operations research staff is not expected to take
over the administrative function. In most cases there are human
aspects of politics or morale which cannot yet be quantified and
which the manager must supply from his experience. Sometimes
these human factors tend to modify the quantitative aspects and
occasionally to negate their implications. Nevertheless, the
process of quantifying what can be so expressed helps to clarify
the nature of the decision to be made; the manager then knows
how much it will cost to let the human aspects overrule the
purely quantitative implications. For this to work effectively,
the operations research team must be in close touch with top
administration; each half of the partnership must have trust

in the other's competence and integrity.

Sometimes the operational problem is solved by a re-examination of past data from a quantitative point of view. For example,[5] an examination of the records of ship collisions in the Skaggerak plus an intensive study of radar tracks of ships in space and time brought out that collisions were much more likely to occur when three ships were near together than when only two were close. The result seems obvious once it is pointed out, for maritime rules are devised for two ships meeting, not for three; but it was not discovered until the data were collected and examined with this in mind. The conclusions also are obvious: In regions of high density, where three-ship encounters begin to be frequent, maritime rules of passage for the three-ship case must be devised and enforced.

At other times the operations research team acts as a sort of feedback control for the administration, finding out what is actually going on and comparing it with what management believes is or should be going on, so that management can issue orders to rectify the discrepancy in behavior or else can revise their plans and estimates to conform more closely to actuality. Sometimes the determination of actual behavior involves the use of specially designed equipment; sometimes it requires the analysis of large amounts of data by an electronic computer.

A Traffic Commissioner, for example, lays out a new set of rules for traffic control, including zoning for parking, phasing of traffic lights, and designation of one-way streets. Are the rules being followed or are only some of them being put into effect? Are the new rules self-consistent or do they conflict with some which were not changed, or with habitual procedures of traffic police? If some peripheral inconsistency is causing confusion, the new set of rules is not necessarily all wrong. But if the Commissioner is not aware of the details of the actual operation, he may conclude that the new system as a whole is at fault. Certainly no realistic decision for change can be made if the administration does not know what is going on. The operations research team often assists in this self-analysis.

The Use of Electronic Computers. When dealing with large and complex systems, the operations research group often involves the assistance of a high-speed computing machine. In many cases the operation is too complicated to be able to be expressed in a system of equations which can be solved with paper and pencil. In these cases a computer can often be programmed to simulate the operation's behavior, with all the important inter-relations and variabilities represented by computer actions. Rather than being a mathematical model, the simulation is a computer model of the system's behavior; it

can be adjusted to fit the actual operation to as detailed a degree
or to as rough an approximation as seems desirable and feasible.
Instead of trying out a new plan of operation with the real flesh-
and-blood system, the plan can be tried out on the simulation;
it is usually much quicker, and certainly there is less at stake
if the plan is a failure.

Traffic engineers are using simulations of automobile flow to
study traffic control in cities. A study for the Port of New York
Authority of the flow of cars through vehicular tunnels by means
of simulations[4] is outlined in Section 1.3. The team experimenting with the simulation did not need to worry if one of their
simulated experiments produced an increase of rear-end collisions -- collisions in the simulation were just a series of red
lights on the computer switchboard.

Computer simulation is also used in city planning. Demographic growth, public and private building, and traffic loads
can be combined, together with their interactions and reactions
to economic trends, to be programmed into the computer so
that it will simulate the urban growth in response to assumed
amounts of subsidy, road building, public housing, and industrial development, for example. A very elaborate forecast[8] of
the growth of Oslo, to be mentioned in Section 1.3, was recently
made in this way and is an excellent example of this technique.
Other examples of the usefulness of computer simulation are
given in later Chapters.

Its Use in Public Affairs. Operations research has only
recently been applied to the problems of public affairs. The
delay is not surprising, for public operations are usually more
complex and involve more purely human aspects than do industrial or military operations. Only recently have the techniques
of operations research been capable of handling such problems.
Also, it has taken longer for the public administrator to realize
that operations research could help him in his administrative
task. Since operations research does not advance in the absence
of close cooperation with the administrator, such a lack of
desire for help has meant that no progress has been possible.

But in the past five years there have been a number of successful applications to operations in the public sector, some of
which are reported in later Chapters. Applications in the field
of traffic control and transportation planning have been mentioned above. Good work in this field is being carried out in
several countries, Norway, the United States, France, and
England, to name a few.[8,9] The studies in urban and regional
planning in France have been outstanding; good work is also
going on in England and in Norway.

The field of public health is a promising one for application,
as indicated in a later Chapter. Here, work is just beginning.

I am persuaded that it can be of great value to hospital administrators as well as to Boards of Health. The problems of education, of the operation of a school system, have had very
little study by O. R. techniques, though some aspects offer
promise of handsome pay-offs.

1.2 Operations Research Procedures

Operations Research is an experimental science; its mathematical model of an operation must be based on quantitative
observation of that operation. For this reason the O. R. man
must have close contact with the participants in the operation,
from manager to laborer, particularly at the beginning of the
study. He must arrange it so that each echelon in the organization will treat him as a friend and helper rather than as a
spy to be fobbed off with partial answers. In this way he can
begin to learn from the manager the policy requirements and
the management problems in meeting the requirements and,
from the lower echelons, the degree of understanding of the
orders which reach them and the operational problems arising
from their execution.

The Importance of Observation. This is not to say that the
O. R. man should view the operation entirely through the eyes
of its participants. It is a common misconception of management, when first dealing with O. R. people, to expect that they
can work in a back office, with data and questions handed to
them. This gives rise to the usual, well-meaning offer of
cooperation, "why take the time to go out to see what goes on;
we'll tell you about it and we'll get other participants to come
in and tell you the details." A practically universal rule is
that participants in an operation cannot give an outsider a
balanced picture of the operation as a whole. Each person,
even the manager, expands his part and distorts those of the
others. Even more misleading is the natural tendency to remember the unusual and to forget the habitual, with the result
that the O. R. man is likely to wind up trying to correct what
happens once a month instead of working to improve what
happens every day. The only safeguard against this error is
for the O. R. man to see for himself, to observe what the participant does, in addition to hearing what he says he does.
Conversation with participants is needed to understand their
attitudes and reactions, which are often important factors in
themselves; observation of actions is necessary to obtain a
quantitative picture of what actually goes on.

Measures of Effectiveness. Early in the investigation the
O. R. worker must begin to formulate quantitative measures of
effectiveness for the operation, measures of the output which

management does, or should, or might, wish to maximize or
minimize.[1] These measures are easiest to formulate for the
simpler industrial operations; the per-unit cost of inventory
or the ratio between the output of a machine and the cost of its
maintenance are examples. In larger systems, particularly
those in the public sector, the measures are not so easy to
formulate and there may be several mutually contradictory
ones. For instance, should automobile traffic through a network be regulated to minimize the time per trip or to maximize
the trips per accident? Should the drug dispensary of a hospital
be operated to maximize the speed of supply or to minimize the
number of mistakes? In cases such as this, alternative solutions are often required, with the several measures calculated
for each solution, so that management can see quantitatively
how much one measure is worsened when another one is
improved.

In many cases the determination of appropriate measures of
effectiveness are further complicated because the manager has
never tried to formulate his standards in quantitative terms.
In determining optimal inventories for a store to carry, for
example, one must balance the cost of maintaining the inventory
against some penalty one assesses the store for the customer's
disappointment in finding an item out of stock. It is very seldom
one finds a manager who is willing to put a number to such a
penalty, even though he is willing to agree that such a penalty
should be charged and that the balancing procedure is a logical
way of calculating optimal inventory.

In these cases it is not necessary to give up, saying that the
problem is too complex; it is better to use an approximate
figure than to get no result. Many times an approximate figure
can be obtained by indirect means. In the case of the out-of-
stock penalty, for instance, it is often possible to get the manager to estimate the maximum fraction of times the item could
be out of stock, above which level he would feel the store was
doing badly. One can then work the inventory model backward
and see what out-of-stock penalty would result in the prescribed
fraction of out-of-stock times. This indirect determination can
often be checked for reasonableness; if the out-of-stock penalty
comes out to be a hundredth of the selling price of the item, or
a hundred times the price, then one would question either the
manager's estimate or the mathematical model, or both. But
if the measure comes out a reasonable size (such as five times
the cost of the item in our example) then one can feel some
confidence in both model and value and proceed to use the
estimated value in other parts of the calculation.

Working Against Time. The operations research worker is
usually trying to help the administrator to reach as wise a

decision as possible, not to devise as accurate a model as he can. Frequently, the decision must be made next month, not five years from now, so the amount of data collection and the accuracy of the calculations must be cut to fit the time schedule. A highly accurate finding presented a month after the administrative decision has been made is worth precisely zero to the administrator. Hence, an estimated value of some measure of effectiveness which may be 50 per cent in error is far better than no estimate.

Furthermore, this may be accurate enough anyway. In a large number of cases, improvement by factors of two may be expected, so accuracies no better than 30 to 50 per cent are allowable. In fact, too great a concentration on accuracy at first may bring out so many minor details that the major effects may be missed. If some measure is to be maximized, the maximum is usually broad. Even if the measure used is somewhat in error, thus suggesting a maximum somewhat displaced from the true maximum, the result will still be near-maximum. Likewise, even if there are large absolute errors in the predicted results when the results of two alternative plans are calculated, the error in the comparison may be much less than the absolute error if the two calculations are made in a comparable manner. Thus the choice between plans is still correctly made.

The comments of the previous paragraph are not an argument for sloppy data-gathering; they are, however, a caution against blind and exhaustive data-collecting. Data that are collected without specific purpose are usually of little future use. In starting a new problem, after the preliminary discussions with participants at all levels and after the initial observation of the activity, the O.R. worker next needs to begin to formulate his model of the operation, to postulate what the important factors are and how they depend on each other. His first data-gathering, then, must be to check out the model, to see whether his guesses are correct; it need only be extensive enough and accurate enough to show that he is on the right track. If the assumed model does not check out, he must try another; if it does appear to be right, then his next data-gathering and analysis should be to improve the model and to estimate the variability of the various components.

Taking Variability into Account. Most of the quantities involved -- for example, degree of demand, times of delivery, rates of arrival, and the like -- are highly variable. Average values are usually not sufficient to predict outcomes; variance, as well as average values, or else the whole distribution of values, is required to specify the appropriate model. If the distribution turns out to correspond to one of the standard

forms, such as normal or Poisson,[2,6] this fact often gives one
insight regarding the operation. To show, for instance, that
arrivals of customers or cars or shipments is Poisson-
distributed in time, will suggest a randomness that has many
implications regarding the model being constructed.

Usually these preliminary data cannot easily be obtained from
the records habitually gathered by the organization. The com-
troller's staff in a business, for example, collects figures to
satisfy particular financial and legal requirements which rarely
coincide with the needs of the O. R. worker. Indeed, the collection methods used by the comptroller, developed for his peculiar
tasks, are often inefficient or inadequate to gather the data to
check out the O. R. model. This is often a source of misunder-
standing at the beginning of a study and may require some
persuasion and educational effort if the situation precludes
data-gathering by the O. R. team itself.

Simple Examples of Data Analysis. Sometimes the conception
of the model plus the confirming data-analysis are sufficient to
solve the operational problem, as was the case in the study of
ship collisions in the Skaggerak mentioned earlier. A second
example of drawing simple conclusions when the data are appropriately analyzed comes from experience in U. S. submarine
operations in the Pacific against Japanese shipping in World
War II. When on the surface, our submarines used radar to
locate the shipping; it gave them an advantage of more than
three in range of sighting ships, and thus enabled them to contact some ten times as many ships per mission; it also made it
much easier for them to accomplish the submerged approach
and attack. But the word soon went around that our radar was
"heard" by the Japanese, that many more Japanese aircraft
attacked our submarines when they used radar, and thus that
we should not use it.

Since turning our radar off meant reducing the effectiveness
of our submarines by a factor of ten, it was important to test
the correctness of the reports that radar "attracted" more
Japanese aircraft. Analysis of the mission reports indicated
that more Japanese aircraft were indeed sighted when radar
was on than when it was off; comparing results in similar locations, the average ratio was approximately four. However,
while there were about four times more sightings, there were
not four times as many actual attacks, since the submarines
were able to submerge sooner and to hide; in fact, there was
no positive evidence that there were any more actual attacks
when radar was on than when it was off. Furthermore, the
sighting records plus some tests then performed at Pearl Harbor
showed that the "range of vision" for Japanese planes, the distance at which the plane was first sighted, was twice as great

for radar as it was for visual sighting by an observer on deck.
Thus, with radar the submarine could survey an area two
squared, or four times as great as it could survey visually.
The increase of four in the sightings was not due to radar
attracting Japanese planes; the submarines could just "see"
farther. If the Japanese had a radar-listening device, it
wasn't doing them any good, so our radar need not be shut off.

1.3 Operational Experiments and Computer Simulation

In many other cases, of course, the solution is not so
straightforward; the measures of effectiveness are not so simple; and more detailed analysis is necessary. After the mathematical model is developed, it may be that appropriate values
of the parameters in the equations must be determined in order
to predict future results. Sometimes this requires operational
experiments: New procedures must be tried out to see their
effect; demand must be changed or rules of operation modified
and the outcome observed. Full-scale operational experiments
are costly and sometimes dangerous, and management is
usually reluctant to authorize them. This is particularly true
in public affairs; experimenting with traffic by obstructing
roads or changing speed limits, for example, is likely to
result in accidents.

Therefore, much operational experimenting must be done
indirectly. Sometimes external effects -- changes in demand
or the introduction of newly built roads, for instance -- can
provide the necessary tests if the effects of these changes are
observed carefully. Sometimes the model predicts large effects
in some unimportant part of the behavior; an experimental
check of this prediction will not be detrimental to the operation
as a whole, but will help indicate the correctness of the model.
Thus, experiment and theory should proceed together.

Simulating Urban Traffic Flow. Often the electronic computer
is of considerable assistance. In the first place, it can be used
to store data in ways that will allow rapid analysis. In the study
of automobile traffic[8] in Oslo, Norway, mentioned earlier, data
on traffic densities and on origin-destination statistics were
recorded in machine-readable form; they could be stored directly on computer tape without costly and error-producing trans-
cription. The data were then analyzed in a number of ways in
order to predict the effect on traffic of possible urban developments, public housing, and new industry, and the effect on
urban development of new highway construction, so that the
results of various plans for urban development could be predicted. The computer enabled a large number of alternative combinations to be worked out without long delays and excessive
cost. Later Chapters in this book by Wolfe and Ernst and by

Loubal give other examples of the use of computers in urban planning.

Inventory Systems. In other cases the computer can be programmed to simulate the operation; the model is a computer model rather than a mathematical one. Rules of operation are programmed in, variability of demand and other factors can be included, and the pertinent results can be printed out in a form familiar to the manager. With a high-speed computer, many trial runs can be made in a short time; a year's experience can be run off in a few minutes.

The behavior of complex inventory systems[3,10] can be simulated in this way, with possible fluctuations in demand, variability in replenishment deliveries, and all the rules of reorder points and transfer from one warehouse to another included. Once the behavior of the computer model is checked against last year's experience, for example, it can be run to predict next year's behavior in case demand changes or inventory levels are increased or some other operating rule is modified.

Tunnel Traffic Flow. These procedures are actually surrogate experiments; instead of experimenting on the actual operation, the computer model is used, with considerable reduction of cost and danger. Of course, one must take pains to ensure that the computer program corresponds closely in its pertinent behavior to the actual operation. In the simulation of one-lane automobile traffic[4] in a vehicular tunnel, mentioned earlier, the dynamic properties of each car, its acceleration and braking properties, and the variations of the properties from car to car were programmed in. In addition, the results of extensive experiments at the General Motors Proving Grounds were used to determine the way in which a driver follows a car ahead of him, the space he prefers to have between cars as a function of speed, the driver and car reaction to changes of speed and spacing, and the variability of these driver-characteristics. All this was also programmed in so that the dynamic behavior of a stream of cars was simulated in all its details and variabilities. Then the overall behavior of the simulated stream was computed for some standard situations and checked against data taken in the Holland Tunnel in New York.

Once the overall behavior of the simulation was checked against the actual behavior of one-lane traffic in a variety of situations, it could be used to see what traffic would do in abnormal situations. Extremes could be tried out, because rear-end collisions in a simulation only gave rise to red lights on the computer console, not to a series of dented fenders and irate drivers. In this case, simulated experimentation with periodic, short-time traffic interruptions predicted possible improvements in overall throughput under conditions of heavy

traffic, with an additional reduction in collision danger. After
this surrogate trial, it was recommended that the procedure be
tried out in actual tunnel traffic. It was put into effect by the
Port of New York Authority and the predicted improvements
were obtained in practice.

Cautionary Comments. These examples show some of the
advantages of using computer simulation as a substitute for
actual operational experiment; they also imply the dangers of
the procedure. Like any other model, the computer model will
not predict correct results unless it corresponds to the actual
operation in all important respects. Often, the complexity of
the programming induces the analyst to feel that complexity
can substitute for realism. The temptation is to insert a sub-
routine because the operational element "ought to behave" in
such-and-such a way, without checking to see whether it does.
The traffic simulation would have been a very questionable procedure without the data on drivers' car-following habits. In
fact, the simulation was not fully checked out until its overall
behavior was checked against actual traffic behavior in a few
cases. Unless realism is built into the details of the program
and unless the whole simulation is checked for normal behavior,
the computer model is only a complicated and impressive way
of making an unverified guess. With appropriate safeguards,
however, the machine simulation is a technique of operational
experiment which is rapidly gaining in scope and usefulness.

The Chapters which follow describe a few examples of the
application of operations research to various operations in the
public sector. Because work in this sector is just beginning,
they are fragmentary samples -- indications of opportunities
rather than textbook examples. It is hoped that they will suggest to the public administrator the kinds of problems which
operations research can help to solve, and that they will indicate to the operations research professional the nature and
scope of the opportunities in this area for the application of his
skills.

1.4 The Role of the Administrator

As implied in the beginning of this Chapter, the payoff for
the research lies in the action of the administrator; in a very
real sense, the results depend on the partnership of effort
between the administrator and his O.R. team. In general, this
partnership works most smoothly if the administrator has his
own team which is continually studying the system he controls
and is anticipating the decisions he will have to be making in
the near future. This is now the case in military staffs and in
many industries; perhaps it will eventually be the case in the
public domain. But at present there are few public administra-

tors who have their own O.R. teams. The question therefore
arises, how can work be started, how can the public administrator organize or find a team to give him the sort of assistance
we have been describing?

Use of Consulting O.R. Teams. Such a team is not easy to
collect. It must include specialists in many disciplines --
mathematicians, economists, engineers, social scientists,
computer programmers, and others -- and these people must
have experience in working together. Unless the unit of government is very large, it is difficult to assemble such a group to
work exclusively for the single unit; even as large a city as
Boston or San Francisco would find it hard, perhaps impossible,
to have such a group working for itself alone. Indeed, most of
the studies reported in this volume have been carried out by
consulting groups which carry out studies for many different
clients. Thus, the pattern of operations research in the field
of public service is one of calling in the expert team, whether
it be a private consulting firm or a group supported by the central government, to do the majority of the work.

But just because the city or other public-service administration has come to rely on an expert consulting team to carry out
the details of the initial study, doesn't mean that there is nothing
for the administration to do. The administrator and his staff
have certain duties and actions with respect to the study and
its implementation which they must carry out, or the whole
procedure will produce no result and the cost of the study will
have been wasted. This need for participation of the administration in the study is so important that it should be spelled out
in detail.

The minimal amount of participation required of the administrator and his staff is threefold: First, the management of the
company or city must conclude that they have problems which
need O.R. analysis; second, the administrative staff must be
sufficiently convinced of the importance of the analysis to be
willing to assist in the gathering of data; and third, both management and its staff must be willing to listen to the results of
the analysis and, if they agree with the findings, to act in accord
with the recommendations.

It often takes a fair amount of work and thought to formulate
the problem, to determine that some part of the system's operation or some aspect of the plans for future operation would be
improved by an operations research analysis. If the city or
other public service is large enough to afford it, there can be
an officer of the administration, a sort of science advisor to
the mayor or to the director, who knows enough about the workings of the system and also knows enough about the techniques
of operations research to be able to locate the places where

such analysis can help. He often will not have the time or the
special knowledge to do the analysis, to solve the problem, but
he can call attention to the problem and suggest that help is
needed to solve it. Even if there is not a specially delegated
"science advisor," there often is a member of the administrative staff with enough technical experience to be able to formulate the problem and to recommend that a study be carried out
to solve it.

It will seldom be the case that all the talents required to make
the analysis are already present in the administrative staff.
Present practice is to call in a consulting group, either a commercial consulting firm or a governmentally supported group
available to many parts of the government, or a group in a
university organized to carry on such consulting work.

Cooperation is Required. But a consulting group of this sort
cannot solve the problems of the city or the agency by themselves; they need to be called in and they must be assisted.
Someone in the organization has to decide that there is a problem and that its solution is important enough to be worth spend-
ing some money to get it solved. And after the group has been
called in, they cannot do the job by themselves. Many people
in the agency or city staff must help in gathering the data needed
for the analysis, and several members of the staff must become
partners in the analysis so that they can inform the consulting
team about details of the system's operations and, more important, so that they can understand the details of the team's
analysis and conclusions.

If the city or agency has only a written report to show for
the money it has paid a consulting team, the chances are that
the report will not be effectively utilized and that the money
has been wasted. A report is not a successful solution of an
operational problem. The true success, the implementation
of the recommendations, is much more likely if, in addition to
the report, a few members of the administrative staff have
worked closely with the consulting team so that they understand
the main outlines of the analysis and the reasons for the conclusions. In a large organization, of course, the science advisor
or his assistant would be the one to work closely with the consulting team; but even if there is no such science advisor, it
is usually possible -- and always desirable -- to find someone
in the staff who can work closely enough with the consultants to
be their interpreter after they have gone.

A plan or a recommendation for action is not worth much
until it is put into practice. And the putting into practice usually
requires much ingenuity and a thorough understanding of what
is important and what is peripheral. Special difficulties always
come up during implementation; they may indicate minor

omissions in the plan which can be corrected with little modification of the whole, or they may be signs that there is some
basic error. Unless there is understanding of the analysis, a
plan which is basically sound may be discarded because of a
minor discrepancy.

The succeeding Chapters in this book will discuss a wide
variety of studies, some of them large-scale and complex,
looking ahead tens of years, others short-range, aimed at
improving a small part of the public service. In every case,
the results have been or will be successful only when the consulting group of experts left behind them understanding and
agreement among the administrative staff in addition to a report
which could be put away in a filing cabinet.

What this means, of course, is that as soon as the public
administrator has decided on the need for a large-scale operations research study to be made by a consulting organization,
he should at the same time plan to organize a small group in
his own staff to monitor the implementation of the study. It
also means that the best way -- indeed perhaps the only way --
to start building this "in-house" group is to assign one or two
appropriate members of one's own staff to work closely with
the consulting group. After this specialized training, these
staff members will automatically be the nucleus of one's own
operations research team, capable of following the plan, of
modifying it if necessary, and of calling for further detailed
study if required later.

This "in-house" group may later be expanded if the work
increases and may, if circumstances permit, become an expert
group which can carry out further studies on its own initiative.
In practice, this procedure seems to be the way operations
research teams are usually formed, particularly in new areas
of application.

References

1. Ackoff, R. L., Progress in Operations Research, John
    Wiley and Sons, Inc., New York, 1961.

2. Fry, T. C., Probability and Its Engineering Uses, D. Van
    Nostrand Co., Inc., New York, 1928.

3. Galliher, H. P., "Ordnance Logistics Studies, II. Secondary
    Item Supply Control," Interim Technical Report No. 9,
    Operations Research Center, M.I.T., Cambridge, Mass.
    (August, 1958).

4. Helly, W. H., "Dynamics of Single-Lane Vehicular Traffic
    Flow," Research Report No. 2, Operations Research
    Center, M.I.T., Cambridge, Mass. (October, 1959).

5. Jensen, A., "Safety at Sea Problems," Paper C-1-10,
    Fourth International Conference on Operational Research,
    August, 1966. To be published in the Proceedings of the
    International Federation of Operational Research Societies.
    This paper outlines the process of solution of this problem
    and also contains interesting comments on the importance
    of new approaches in the formulation of an operational
    problem.

6. Machol, R., <u>System Engineering Handbook</u>, McGraw-Hill
    Book Co., New York, 1965. Chapters 28 and 38.

7. Morse, P. M., and G. E. Kimball, <u>Methods of Operations</u>
    <u>Research</u>, John Wiley and Sons, Inc., New York, 1951.

8. Oslo Byplan-Kontor, <u>Transportanalysen for Oslo-Omradet,</u>
    Kirstes Boktrykkeri, Oslo, Norway, 1965.

9. SEMA (Societe d'Economie et de Mathematique Appliquees),
    "Etude de l'Armature Urbaine" (<u>Region Bretagne,</u>
    December, 1965; <u>Region Poitou-Charentes,</u>, December,
    1965; <u>Pays de la Loire</u>, January, 1966), Paris, France.

10. Simond, M. M., "Control and Simulation of a Variable-
    Demand Supply System," Interim Technical Report No. 7,
    Operations Research Center, M.I.T., Cambridge, Mass.
    (July, 1957) (adaptation).

11. Smith, B.L.R., <u>The RAND Corporation</u>, Harvard Univer-
    sity Press, Cambridge, Mass., 1966. Chapters 5 and 6.

Chapter 2

OPERATIONAL RESEARCH IN LOCAL GOVERNMENT[*]

R. A. Ward

2.1 Introduction

This Chapter begins by giving some idea of the way in which
operational research into the problems of local government has
been supported in the author's own country, the U.K.[2] The
Local Government Operational Research Unit had its origin in
a research project sponsored by the Royal Institute of Public
Administration in 1959 to examine the potential usefulness of
operational research to local authorities. By 1964, it became
evident that operational research could be of value to local
authorities in a variety of ways, some of which were described
in a book published in that year.[5]

It also became clear that operational research could be most
effectively undertaken for local authorities by a central organization. Only a relatively small number of people have the apti-
tude and capacity for the kind of work involved, with the result
that operational research scientists are scarce and must be
deployed in the way that makes the best use of them. Also,
research into new problems is bound to be time-consuming and
expensive, but once solutions have been found, they can usually
be applied quite widely with much less time and effort.

With a number of simple exploratory studies completed, it
was possible to present to Local Authorities in Britain the idea
of forming such a central Unit on a permanent basis. At a conference in November, 1964 representatives from over 100 of
Britain's larger Authorities were drawn together for a day to
examine how this might be done.

Membership was offered initially to the major Local Authorities, and they were invited to join a consortium to support the
development of the Unit. The Unit's objectives were defined as
follows: (1) to undertake studies by operational research methods to assist Local Authorities in their policy and management
decisions; (2) to make known the results of those studies as

[*] This Chapter is adapted from R. A. Ward's Operational
Research in Local Government, by permission of the
publishers, Royal Institute of Public Administration, London.

17

widely and as quickly as possible, and to give such assistance
as may be necessary to the member authorities who wish to
introduce them; (3) to co-operate with other bodies, research
associations, and universities in fields related to local government services.

The authorities consulted were the governing councils of each
of 62 counties and 84 county boroughs. Of these, some 35 of
the former and 40 of the latter have supported the work of the
Unit. Counties contain both urban and rural areas, and their
councils have control over such matters as education, highways,
police, libraries, welfare, and fire service. Certain other
functions, such as refuse collection and public transport are
controlled by district authorities, districts being county sub-
divisions. County boroughs are urban areas with population
over 75,000, and their councils have control over all the matters listed above.

Each of the Authorities served by the Unit pays a small share
of the cost, with the central government planning to contribute
an additional 40 per cent. The staff presently consists of 20
members trained in such areas as physics, mathematics,
sociology, economics, and psychology. Thus the Local Government Operational Research Unit was formally established in
1965. Several diverse examples of the Unit's work will now be
given.

2.2 Buying Policy and Inventory Control[5]

The first problem we shall discuss is one which was investigated prior to 1964; it concerns inventory policy for government
warehouses. The financial efficiency of a warehouse depends
very much on the quality of the decisions on buying policy. At
the root of these are the following questions to which the right
answers must be found:

1. Whether to hold a particular item in stock or to buy it as
   and when required.
2. When to place orders for items held in stock.
3. How much to buy when reordering, including consideration
   of possible discounts for bulk orders.

In analyzing these questions it is convenient to deal with them
in reverse order, and to start with the problem of how much
to buy when reordering.

How Much to Order. Figure 2.1 indicates a range of choices
when reordering. Diagram A indicates the consequences of
placing small orders frequently, in contrast with diagram C,
which illustrates the effects of large orders placed less frequently. Diagram B represents an intermediate policy. The
question to be resolved for each particular commodity is:

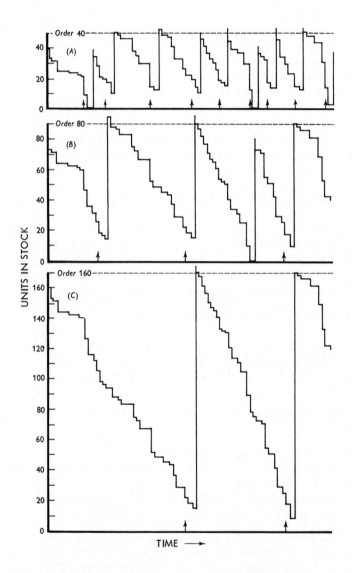

Figure 2.1. Stock records with replacement orders of various sizes.

Which policy is least costly?

With example A the quantity of goods in stock at any one time
will be small, and the storage space required and capital tied
up will be correspondingly limited. With example C space and
capital will be required on a larger scale. On the other hand,
in example A many more orders must be placed over a given
period than in example C, and this will involve some expense.
Also, important discounts available on bulk orders may be
forfeited. The problem is, therefore, to find the best balance
between these conflicting factors.

These general considerations will be readily appreciated,
and it is interesting to consider Figure 2.2, derived from the
records of a local authority's building supplies warehouse.

Buying policy in this particular warehouse seems to have
been inconsistent, because of the substantial variations between
the quantities ordered at different times and between the levels
of existing stocks when fresh orders were placed.

A critical question to be considered in detail is the quantity
of a particular commodity to be purchased when an order is
placed and, in arriving at that decision, it is necessary to
recognize that some costs will increase as the size of the orders
is enlarged, and that others will decrease. The following are
among those which will increase with the size of the order:

1. Annual cost of providing storage space.
2. Interest on the money tied up on stocks.
3. Annual loss due to deterioration or obsolescence (i.e.,
   stock written off).
4. Annual loss from holding stocks during a period of falling
   prices.

The following costs will decrease as the size of the order is
increased:

5. Annual cost of placing orders.
6. Annual gain from holding stocks during a period of rising
   prices -- the alternative to (4).
7. Annual gain which can be achieved by bulk discounts or
   special delivery rates.

All these factors, except bulk discounts, will vary either in
direct or inverse proportion to the size of orders which are
placed and, in reaching a decision on each commodity, it is
necessary to know what the combined effects of these factors
are on different sizes of orders. It is in assessing the combination of these effects that the operational research scientist
can be helpful. He can develop an equation of warehouse costs
containing the following factors:

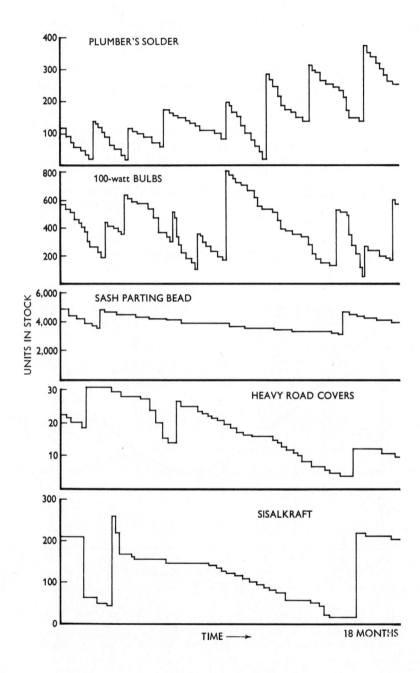

Figure 2.2. Examples of actual stock records.

| Total annual cost of running the warehouses | = | Annual cost of providing storage space | + | Interest on money tied up in stocks | + | Annual loss due to obsolescence and deterioration |

$$+ \quad \text{Annual administrative cost of replacing stocks} \quad + \quad \text{Annual gain or loss from changing price levels}$$

The five factors on the right-hand side of this equation will depend on the size of the orders placed, but the extent to which each of them will affect the total may differ with each order size.

With this equation it is possible by mathematical means to work out the total annual cost of running the warehouses for a range of order sizes from the smallest to the largest and, when this is done for any selected commodity, the kind of graph shown in Figure 2.3 is obtained. The left-hand side of the

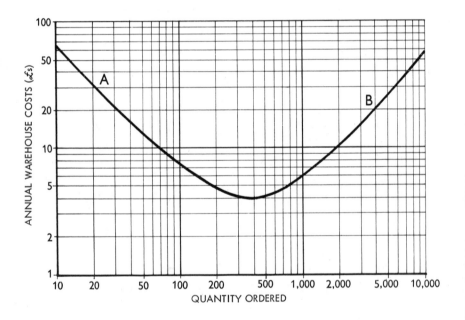

Figure 2.3. Graph of the equation of warehouse costs.

graph shows the relatively high cost which arises from the frequent ordering of small quantities, while the right-hand side indicates the high costs which have to be met when large quantities are ordered at long intervals. It is apparent from this graph that, for the commodity in question, the lowest storage cost is reached when the replacement order is 380 units.

The graph in Figure 2.3 has not taken account of possible
bulk discounts. It will be seen from that graph that the annual
storage cost of buying 1,000 at a time would be £2 a year more
than buying 380. The discount would be worth obtaining, therefore, only if it amounted to more than £2 a year by buying
1,000 at a time. Thus, in this way, it is possible to ascertain
the appropriate quantity to order for any particular item. Conversely, an indication can be obtained of the minimum discount
that must be negotiated in order to justify bulk orders of particular   sizes above the order quantity involving the minimum cost.

   The Practical Application. Since it would obviously be pro-
hibitively expensive to have to follow these successive procedures for each item in the warehouse, it is necessary to devise
a system which can enable the required decisions to be obtained
automatically as far as possible. The following paragraphs
accordingly describe how, for this purpose, a special ready
reckoner can be constructed. Such a ready reckoner must take
account of the five factors indicated on the right of the equation
of warehouse costs. Particularly important are the following
variable elements which affect these factors, because they tend
each to be different for every commodity:

1. The annual cost of storing each unit.
2. The expected annual consumption.
3. The price of each unit of the commodity.

The facts in regard to (2) and (3) will be known already, or will
be easily ascertainable. Item (1) constitutes more of a problem
because of the very wide range of sizes occupied by units of different commodities. It is practicable, however, to classify all
commodities according to their bulk, and thus to place them in
a series of storage costs. For example, in a housing warehouse depot it is reasonable to have five categories based on
the annual costs for storing one unit of a particular commodity
of £.0001, £.001, £.01, £0.1, and £1. A washer would come
in the first category and a bath tub in the last.

   For each category of storage cost it becomes practicable to
prepare a chart which deals with the variable elements -- (2)
expected annual consumption, and (3) price of each unit -- and
demonstrates the optimum quantity of a particular commodity
to be purchased according to all the relevant factors indicated
in the equation of stores costs. Table 2.1 illustrates such a
chart.

   It will be seen that selected figures have been taken for
annual consumption and for prices, since it is clearly imprac-
ticable to quote every conceivable value over the necessary
range. The chart is used by taking the nearest figures of
consumption and price for the commodity in question, and then

Table 2.1. Order Quantity Chart

UNIT COST OF STORAGE £.1 p.a.   ORDERING COST £.43   RATE OF INTEREST 6%
INFLATION AND DETERIORATION OF 0%

QUANTITY TO ORDER IF NO DISCOUNTS AVAILABLE

Cost of Each Unit			NUMBER OF UNITS USED PER YEAR																
£	s.	d.	1	2	5	10	15	30	60	100	250	500	1,000	1,500	3,000	5,000	8,000	10,000	15,000
		1	5	6	10	15	17	24	36	45	74	107	154	173	248	317	404	455	550
		3	5	6	10	15	17	24	35	45	73	106	153	172	247	316	402	454	548
		6	5	6	10	15	17	24	35	44	73	106	152	171	245	314	396	451	535
		9	4	6	10	15	17	24	34	44	72	104	151	169	240	310	388	446	528
	2	6	4	6	9	14	16	23	33	42	68	99	147	160	230	294	375	422	520
	5	0	4	6	9	13	15	21	31	39	64	93	134	150	215	276	352	396	490
	8	0	4	5	8	12	13	19	28	35	58	84	121	136	195	250	319	359	440
	16	0	3	4	7	10	12	17	24	31	50	73	105	118	169	216	276	311	380
1	10	0	3	4	6	8	10	14	20	25	41	60	87	97	139	178	228	250	320
2	15	0	2	3	5	7	8	11	16	20	33	48	69	78	112	143	183	206	240
5	10	0	2	2	3	5	6	8	12	15	25	36	51	58	83	106	135	152	185
10	0	0	1	1	2	3	3	5	7	9	15	22	31	35	31	65	82	93	110

correspondingly rounding up or down the final figure. Thus,
for a warehouse item costing 5 shillings, of which 500 were
used each year, the chart shows 93 to be the optimum number
to order, and it would be sensible to round this up to 100.

Allowing for Discounts. The system just described takes
account of all the stated factors except that of discounts. These
provide a further dimension to the problem, and to meet this it
is necessary to break down each of the main charts just illustrated, based on the average cost of storing a unit each year,
into a series of such charts, each one referring to a different
annual consumption. Table 2.2 illustrates the new kind of
chart that can be developed to deal with the problem of discounts.

This Table is developed from one column of the earlier chart,
Table 2.1, namely, that shown against an annual consumption
of 60. With a series of charts of this kind there results a book
consisting of about 200 pages. This is in five main parts, one
for each storage category based on the cost of storing one unit
over a year, and each part is broken down on the basis of the
annual consumption of the commodity.

With this book the officer concerned can readily ascertain
the quantity to order, having regard to all the relevant factors,
including the possibility of obtaining discounts for bulk purchases. Thus, for an item costing 16s. of which 60 are used
each year, the best number to order will be two dozen unless,
for example, a discount on the year's supply of at least £4 8s.
is offered for orders of a gross, or at least £20 for orders of
500. Numerous and lengthy mathematical calculations are
involved in preparing this book. Fortunately, however, they
can be done by a modern computer within minutes, and the
mathematician is saved the labor and tedium in which he would
have been involved less than a decade ago. Revision of the
book would become necessary if a large warehouse reorganiza-
tion took place. In the absence of such a change, a review is
probably desirable every two years. The preparation of a
revised book will generally involve very little labor and will
consist mainly of the cost of computer time, which is unlikely
to exceed £50.

This study also went on to examine Problem 2, "When to
place orders for items held in stock," and also Problem 1,
"Whether to hold items in stock or to buy them as and when
required." Unfortunately, space prevents elaborating more
fully on these two further aspects of the warehouse problem.

Since the study was first made, however, a rather deeper
look has been given to the question of whether to stock or buy
direct, and some very interesting new concepts have now
emerged.

There appears to be every reason to believe that these new

Table 2.2. Order Quantity When Discounts Are Available

Take Bulk Discount Only If Its Annual Value Exceeds Figure Given In Body of Table

Annual Demand on Stock

| | | | 60 | | | | | | | |

QUANTITY TO OBTAIN DISCOUNT

PRICE PER UNIT (£ s. d.)	Optimum Order Size	10	12	20	36	50	72	100	144	500
1	36					.1	.4	.9	1.7	8.9
3	35					.1	.4	.9	1.7	9.0
6	35					.1	.4	.9	1.7	9.1
9	34					.1	.5	1.0	1.9	9.8
2 6	33					.1	.5	1.1	2.1	10.5
5 0	31					.2	.6	1.3	2.4	12.1
8 0	28				.1	.3	.9	1.7	3.1	14.9
16 0	24				.2	.6	1.4	2.6	4.4	20.1
1 10 0	20				.5	1.2	2.5	4.2	7.0	30.2
2 15 0	16			.1	1.1	2.3	4.4	7.1	11.5	47.5
5 10 0	12			.6	3.0	5.4	9.3	14.4	22.5	88.4
10 0 0	7	.4	.9	4.1	11.5	18.3	29.1	43.1	65.0	243.1

approaches to warehousing problems will enable a number of important policy issues to be resolved: for example, how big should a warehouse be, or, how much capital does it pay to tie up in stocks. The new methods will enable us to demonstrate the return of capital which the warehousing process is giving and also the value of the space and premises that have been put aside for storage, the important point being that it is now possible to draw a clear distinction between the value of these facilities and their cost.

With this aside, let us now return to the results of the early work which paved the way for this later development.

The Results of Experiments. In the course of practical studies over the last three years, experiments have been carried out at Swindon, first on a small housing warehouse with a turnover of £40,000 a year; more recently on the Engineer's warehouse with a turnover of £70,000 a year; and at Battersea on a general building warehouse with an annual turnover of £55,000. In addition, experiments have been carried out at Coventry on the stationery warehouse, and at the United Kingdom Atomic Energy Authority's main warehouse at Harwell, where the turnover approaches £3 million a year.

One interesting feature to emerge was that in most of the warehouses at least 20 per cent of the commodities stocked were found not to have been issued in the preceding twelve months, and those in charge of the warehouse had not realized that so high a proportion of the stock had remained static.

As a result of these experiments, it is believed that those responsible for the warehouses now have a better understanding of the factors affecting purchasing decisions and of stores control. It is also certain that senior officers concerned with these warehouses have come to recognize that they must define formally the basic policies they wish followed in the running of these warehouses. Indeed, the preparation and use of a ready reckoner of the kind described earlier is such a policy definition. It is also clear that if an operational research inquiry is to be undertaken successfully, the officer responsible for the warehouse must be involved in the development and introduction of the scheme.

Financial savings have undoubtedly been achieved in the inquiries so far completed. First, they have tended to lead to a change in the balance of commodities held in stock. It has been found desirable to hold larger stocks of small and cheap commodities, and to reduce the levels of those which are large in bulk and high in price. Second, those responsible for running the warehouse have come to recognize the need for a keen appreciation of the market and its possibilities. Aided by the information revealed by the ready reckoner, purchasing officers

have been better informed on the quantities and bulk discounts
which it would pay them to obtain and, instead of merely considering an offer made by a supplier without really knowing how
advantageous it is, a purchasing officer can take the initiative
in telling suppliers of the quantities he is prepared to purchase
if sufficiently attractive discounts are available. This has led
to a keener method of seeking tenders. Third, a more precise
understanding of the control information that warehouse administrators need has been revealed. In some instances superflu-
ous clerical procedures have been eliminated, especially where
it has been found possible to maintain one warehouse record for
both costing and control purposes.

The results so far achieved indicate that between 2 per cent
and 4 per cent of the annual value of the warehouse's turnover
can be saved. These savings often take the form of immediate
cash benefits. Thus, in Swindon, for example, savings received
from bulk discounts meant that the annual cost of £6,000 for
operating the warehouse was reduced by 16 per cent. In addition,
a certain amount of storage space was released. In one authority it had been the practice to order cement in quantities of three
or four tons. The new policy showed that savings of £200 a year
would be secured if cement were ordered in eight-ton lots, even
though this involved the construction of a new lean-to shed to
store this larger quantity. In a big warehouse such a decision
may appear self-evident, but when the amounts used are small
the answer is by no means obvious.

As earlier comments indicated, the foregoing methods were
not designed simply to secure piecemeal and marginal savings
of storage space and staff time, but to enable top management
to reach better decisions on broader issues.

The theory underlying the research described here and utilized in the practical experiments was not new to operational
research. The significance of these experiments is that they
mark the introduction of these techniques to local government,
and demonstrate the scope that exists for more powerful methods
of formulating a warehouse policy and of controlling warehouses than those at present employed. If the methods described
in this Chapter were applied to the 400 largest Local Authorities
in the United Kingdom, the aggregate savings would certainly
be very large.

2.3 School Supplies[3]

An interesting development arose when the Unit was asked to
apply stock-control techniques to the ordering of educational
supplies. Demand by the schools showed a large seasonal variation, thus forcing the hiring of excess staff in the Supplies
Department and considerable delivery difficulties during high-

demand periods. Also, extensive stock rooms were needed to store goods for the peak periods. In order to find out why this seasonal work load occurred, a survey was made of the way in which 48 typical schools used their materials.

The results of the survey showed that the seasonal effect was largely a result of the schools' requisitioning procedures, not a reflection of the way in which pupils used materials. The survey also gave data on the size of stores of various items kept in schools, which gave some indication of the hidden cost of supplies borne by the Education and Treasurer's Departments. Thus the problem becomes one of designing an appropriate requisitioning procedure for schools, rather than one of dealing with a costly seasonal demand.

2.4 Degree of Centralization of Warehouses[1]

Work was recently completed on a project which examined the effect of warehouse centralization on the cost of storing major domestic appliances for the South Eastern Electricity Board. Sales of these items run to several millions of pounds annually, and some 400 models are handled. At the start of the study a separate inventory was held in each of 26 districts in a 3,000-square-mile area. This system remained from a time when each district was considered the territory of a separate firm. The question was whether savings could be realized by consolidating these inventories in some way.

Preliminary investigation showed that the problem could conveniently be divided into two portions, one dealing with storage costs and another having to do with the cost of distribution. Each of these costs could be analyzed as a function of the degree of centralization without significantly affecting the other. The basic effects of centralization on these costs were clear: Increasing centralization would reduce storage costs by (a) decreasing aggregate labor forces, (b) allowing more discounts for quantity delivery, (c) decreasing ordering costs because fewer orders need be placed, and (d) decreasing the total "safety stock" kept to insure continuity of supply. On the other hand, increasing centralization would certainly increase the cost of local delivery. It was decided to analyze the specific costs of both storage and delivery for situations in which the number of warehouses was reduced from the present 26 to 10, 5, 3, 2, and 1. For this purpose several mathematical models were constructed, and a high-speed digital computer was employed for most calculations.

The results of this study showed that the increased local delivery costs entailed by high centralization were more than offset by the gains in storage costs and buying advantages. In an attempt to get the best of both worlds, it was decided to

examine a system in which appliances were transported in bulk
from a central warehouse to redistribution points for local delivery. It must be stressed that these redistribution points are
not sub-warehouses but depots where the goods were taken off
one large vehicle and put onto several small ones on a daily
routine. It was found that one central warehouse with three
redistribution points would be most economical, but that the
costs of having 26 redistribution points were not appreciably
greater. Accordingly, a system of one central warehouse and
26 redistribution points was recommended so as to fit the existing district scheme as closely as possible. Annual predicted
savings for this system are on the order of £160,000, and
plans for its implementation are well advanced.

2.5 Invoice Checking[5]

A Supplies Department will receive many invoices to pass
for payment during the course of a year. Traditional account-
ing practice demands that these should all be carefully checked
and, if necessary, rectified before payment. The cost of such
checking can be considerable, however, and experience shows
that a very high proportion of the invoices checked are, in fact,
correct. The question therefore arises whether it would not be
possible to check only a selection of the invoices and to ascertain what savings this would lead to. In making this calculation
the probable cost of undetected errors would have to be taken
into account.

The extreme possibilities are the checking, or even double-
checking, of all invoices and no checking at all. The former
practice may be extravagant in staff and office costs, while the
latter would certainly be financially dangerous. The problem
to be resolved is whether a balance point can be settled between
these two extremes which can produce an overall saving, i.e.,
a direct saving in checking costs which more than offsets any
financial losses resulting from undetected errors. Studies concerning this question have been carried out for several governmental authorities. In these studies, reductions of checking
costs of between 25 and 50 per cent have been found, suggesting
that if all members of the Unit were to adopt sampling procedures, almost a million pounds could be saved annually. The
method of analysis will now be discussed.

The Pattern of Invoice Values. The first step was to ascertain the number of invoices of different values to be paid; the
result is indicated in Figure 2.4. As will be seen, a substantial proportion of the invoices are for small amounts. For
example, 9 per cent of them are for amounts between 10s. and
£1, and 12 per cent between £1 and £2. Invoices for large
amounts occur less frequently, and only 3 per cent fall in the

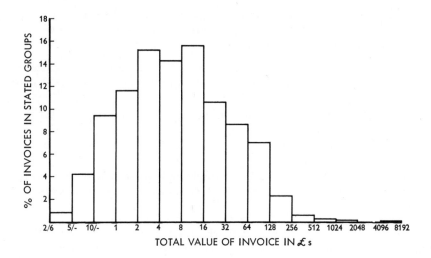

Figure 2.4. The pattern of invoice values.

range £128 to £256.

The pattern can be demonstrated in another way, as shown in Figure 2.5. It will be seen from this that 40 per cent of the invoices are for amounts greater than £12 and that only 10 per cent exceed £64 in value. Each authority will, of course, have its own distinct pattern of invoice values, depending on the nature of its buying policy. In this study about 150,000 invoices with a total value of £3,000,000 were under consideration.

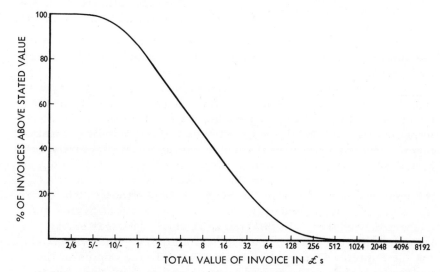

Figure 2.5. Percentage of invoices above various values.

   Types of Check. The next step was to classify the types of
,check inherent in the existing clerical procedures. These were
designed to ensure the following:

1. That the invoice related to an order placed by the authority
   and was not, for example, intended for another purchaser,
   or a duplicate.
2. That a delivery had been made of the goods to which the
   invoice related.
3. That the delivery made was not defective in quality or
   quantity.
4. That the invoice had been made out at the right prices.
5. That the arithmetical calculations on the invoice were
   correct.

In order to ascertain how often queries arose within the categories identified by these checks, the correspondence files for
the previous year were examined in detail. Since the authority
had hitherto been carrying out these checks comprehensively,
it was assumed that all errors of this kind had been detected
and had become the subject of correspondence. This examination revealed the following information:

		%
1. Invoices not appropriate to authority or duplicate invoices		.25
2. No delivery of goods invoiced		.05
3. Delivery defective in quality or quantity		.80
4. Invoice incorrectly priced	Overcharged	.23
	Undercharged	.06
5. Arithmetical errors	Against authority	.076
	For authority	.063

It follows that the proportion of invoices which did not become
the subject of correspondence and were assumed to be correct
was 98.47 per cent.

   Confirmation of Delivery. At least half the detected errors
were thus due to defects in delivery. It had hitherto been the
practice for the officer responsible for the receipt of the goods
to return the copy of the original order to the Supplies Department, indicating whether the order had been satisfactorily completed or, if not, the nature of the fault. Each of these copy
orders had to be attached to the relevant invoice, as well as
the copy order retained in the Supplies Department. These
three documents provided the basis for subsequent paying and
costing procedures. In the course of this investigation, it
became apparent that it would be satisfactory, with one proviso,
for the Supplies Department to receive only the copies of those
orders on which delivery had been defective, and to dispense
with the copies of the orders which had been satisfactorily

completed. This would eliminate the transmission and handling of practically all these documents. The reservation to be made arose from the possibility of payment for goods of which no delivery had been made, since that situation would no longer be distinguishable from one of satisfactory delivery. It was accordingly necessary to examine this source of loss, which amounted to .05 per cent of all the invoices.

The question to be examined was at what level it would pay to obtain a certificate of delivery for the more expensive invoices. On the basis of the different numbers of invoices of different values indicated in Figure 2.4, it was a simple matter to calculate the expected loss arising from this error for each price group of invoices and, when these had been obtained, to express them in the form shown in Figure 2.6. The calculation

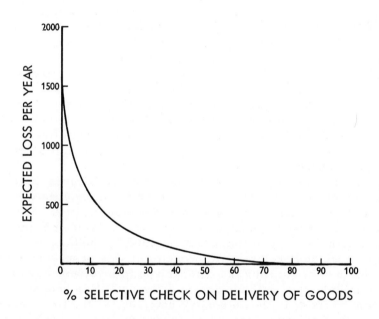

Figure 2.6. Expected losses through failure of delivery at various checking levels.

on which the graph is based assumes that expensive goods are as likely to fail in delivery as are cheap ones. No evidence could be found to contradict this simple assumption. It will be seen that by checking the high-value invoices, which are a small proportion of the whole, appreciable reductions in the losses through failure to deliver can be secured. Thus by checking the top 10 per cent of all invoices, i.e., the most expensive ones, a potential loss of £1,500 a year is reduced

to £600 a year.   To check more than the top 50 per cent, however, will avoid only trivial losses.

Best Level of Checking. Against these considerations must
be set the varying costs of selective checks at different levels.
It must be recognized that checking processes often incorporate
ancillary procedures necessary in the settlement of the invoices
and to meet related accountancy requirements, and that the
elimination of all the checking procedures would not save the
whole of the staff time that is involved in dealing with invoices
for one purpose or another. An analysis was accordingly made
of the time spent by the clerical staff in checking invoices for
the delivery of goods.

These results can be represented graphically by the straight
line in Figure 2. 7, which shows on the left the cost of not checking at all and on the right the cost of 100 per cent checking.
The Figure also incorporates the expected losses from failure
to deliver (copied from Figure 2. 6) and a further curve at the
top indicating the total effect for different selective checks,
i. e. , the combined effect of the other two factors represented.

This shows clearly that the best balance between excessive
checking and losses through paying invoices for goods not delivered is achieved when confirmation of delivery is sought on
only the 10 per cent most expensive invoices. The clerical
cost of £500 at 0 per cent refers to activities not affected by
the amount of checking and has been included to aid the graphical presentation.

Apart from errors due to inadequacies or failures in deliveries, the next most serious error arose from invoices which
had either been incorrectly sent or were duplicates. This
check, as already operated, involves a comparison of the invoice with the copy of the order retained by the Supplies Department to which it refers. An economy in this procedure might
be obtained by limiting the comparison to invoices above a
certain value, as with checks on delivery. This course did not
commend itself to the authority, however, at the time, and no
revision of existing arrangements was proposed in this particular respect.

Checking the Price. With regard to the check on the prices
charged, where . 23 per cent of the invoices had errors against
the authority and . 06 per cent in their favor, it was necessary
to consider not only the numbers of errors which were occurring, but the proportion of the invoice value which they tended
to represent. It was found that errors in price against the
authority formed on average about 13 per cent of the invoice
value, while price errors in favor of the authority averaged
about 10 per cent of the invoice value. This second group of
errors was dominated by the omission of purchase tax that

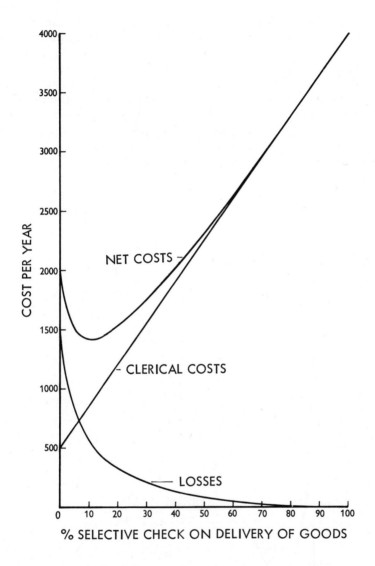

Figure 2.7. The effect of selective checking for receipt of
goods on losses and clerical costs.

should have been charged. After allowing for an adjustment to
these figures to take account of later rectifications that would
have been made through the discovery of the mistakes after payment, the net effect of the price errors on the authority worked
out at .025 per cent of the value of the year's purchases,
namely £750.

Having reached this point it was necessary to find out on
what values of invoices price errors were most frequently

coming to light.   Examination showed that the existing check
on prices was in practice, already being carried out selectively,
and that the higher-value invoices carried more detected errors
than those of lower value.   Since there was no reason to suppose
that the price errors did in fact occur more frequently on the
higher-value invoice, it was assumed that the analysis of the
correspondence had not disclosed all the price errors that could
be expected.   An adjustment for this was made, after which the
losses arising at various points over the total range of possible
selective checks were calculated, producing the diagram of
Figure 2.8.

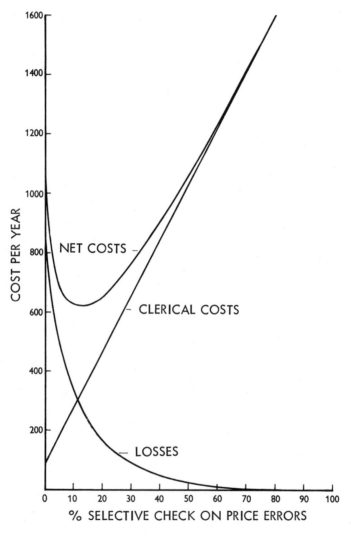

Figure 2.8. Net losses through price errors.

It will be seen that this is very similar to the diagram produced for losses arising from delivery failure (Figure 2. 7) and
that a large portion of these losses can be avoided by checking
a relatively small percentage of the invoices, namely those
with high face value.

The marginal costs of clerical checking for price errors had
to be assessed, and this was done by studying and measuring
the work which it involved. Once again it produced a straight
line which could be combined with the losses arising from net
overcharging. The outcome of this analysis is illustrated in
Figure 2. 8, and shows that the point of lowest overall cost is
obtained by checking the top 12 per cent of all invoices (i. e. ,
the 12 per cent with the highest face value).

Arithmetical Errors. This left only the question of arithmetical errors, which it will be recalled were fairly evenly balanced, . 076 per cent being against the authority and . 063 per
cent being in their favor. Here an experiment was carried out
using the actual errors detected in the course of the year to
show the net effect of limited checks starting with the largest
invoices first. This produced the graph of Figure 2. 9.

It is interesting to note that, if only the top 10-15 per cent of
the invoices are checked, no net loss will result to the authority.
With that degree of selective checking, the authority is in the
same position as if it had carried out a 100 per cent check.
Further, with about a 25 per cent check, it stands to make a
small net gain of about £ 50. There is a simple explanation of
this phenomenon which can be illustrated by an example. Suppose that invoices over £ 50 are to be checked while those under
£ 50 are to be accepted without check. An invoice which should
have been £ 45 but has been overcharged by £ 6 will become
eligible for checking. Conversely, an invoice which should
have been £ 51 but is undercharged by £ 6 will escape scrutiny.
Thus, through selective checking on the basis of face values,
a bias occurs in favor of the authority. The important feature
of the curve in Figure 2. 9 is, however, that relatively heavy
net losses can be avoided by a selective check confined to the
top 10 per cent of the invoices.

It must be mentioned that checking for the detection of arithmetical errors was not a very expensive clerical operation in
this authority. Had the analysis been developed in relation to
marginal checking costs, as with checks for delivery and
pricing, an optimum check of about 30 per cent would probably
have been revealed. However, the desirability of a uniform
standard of checking suggested that a selective check of the
top 12 per cent of all invoices would provide the most practical
and economic answer. The recommended procedure can then
be illustrated in Figure 2. 10.

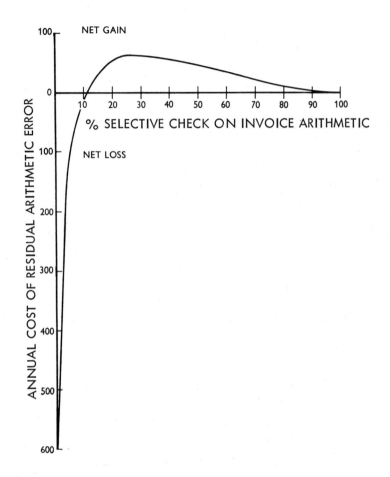

Figure 2.9. Effect of various checking levels on residual
           arithmetical error.

Reliability of the Results. The foregoing analyses were carried out on only one year's records, which might not be typical.
Further, not all the invoices dealt with during the year were
examined, but only the correspondence arising from the detected errors. Should any doubt be entertained, therefore, about
the reliability of the figures which led to the conclusion that a
12 per cent check would be the best? Calculations were accordingly made of the effects of the errors being twice as serious
as the analysis had revealed, e.g., that delivery failures occurred in 0.1 per cent instead of .05 per cent of the cases. The
result of these calculations was to show that checking of the
top 20 per cent of the invoices would have been the optimum
and that the financial losses resulting from the more limited

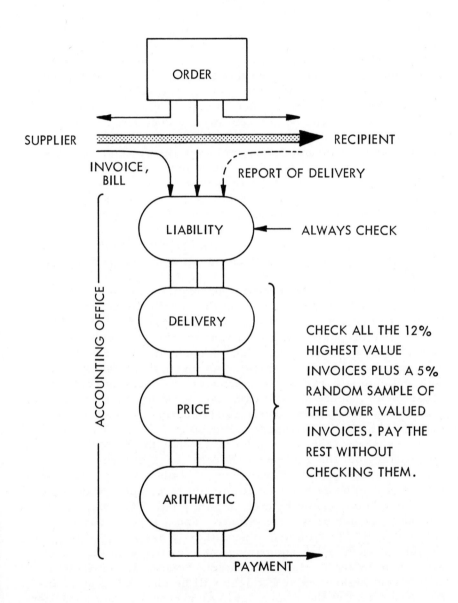

Figure 2.10. Recommended procedure for checking for
       arithmetical errors.

check were likely to be less than £500 a year, and by no means
serious in relation to the total turnover. This demonstration
of the effect of a substantial margin of error in the basic analysis was reassuring to the authority.

Changes of Circumstances and Dangers of Fraud. Two further considerations remained to be dealt with -- the possibility
that circumstances might change, so rendering the original
data obsolete, and the chance that the authority might expose
itself to fraud as a result of the new system of selective checking. It was accordingly decided to make a check of about 5 per
cent of the remaining 88 per cent of invoices, i.e., those below
£60. The purpose of this check is not to correct further errors,
but to provide management control over the system. By this
process of continuous sampling, an assessment can be made of
the frequency and value of the errors which are occurring, so
enabling management to ascertain whether the selective sampling is still being carried out at the level which gives the least
overall cost, and is therefore in need of adjustment.

This random check also provides a safeguard against repetitive small frauds which, although they might escape detection
a few times, would ultimately be brought to light.

A system of selective checking of invoices above a specified
value does, of course, leave open the possibility of fraudulent
attempts to obtain a succession of small payments below that
level. The proposed 5 per cent random check provides against
such a fraud continuing for a long period, and will result in
only one chance in three of losing as much as £1,000 a year in
undetected small frauds. The process of allocating costs to
departments, subsequent to payment, provides another safeguard, however, against such frauds continuing, and the real
risk is therefore substantially reduced.

At first the authority considered whether the Audit Department
might carry out the 5 per cent random check in place of certain
routine inspections which they were already making. This was
not deemed to be an audit function, however, and it was decided
that the scheme should be treated as a single operation involving
a proper balance between a selective and a random check.

Conclusion. To sum up: The authority has retained its
present procedure for comparing each invoice with the copy
order held by the Buying Department. Otherwise, only the
12 per cent highest value invoices will be checked, and a random 5 per cent of the remainder. As a result of this reduction
in checking, the authority may lose almost £800 a year by
error and omission, but will save about £6,000 in clerical
costs. The net saving of £5,200 will be nearly half the total
cost of the work previously involved in passing invoices for
payment.

The idea of sampling is not, of course, new in accountancy, and many authorities have made use of partial checking for some time. The value of this particular study, however, lies in its demonstration of the large amount of checking which can be eliminated with advantage. Some authorities may feel that partial checking disregards the safety of public money. It should be mentioned, therefore, that the Institute's proposals were carefully considered by the Council's Internal Auditor and by the District Auditor, and that these two officers supported the Institute's recommendations when they were submitted to the Council. Sampling procedures are widely used in other public services, notably in Customs and Excise and in air-line operations, where financial settlements are arranged between the air lines on only a sample of their debts to one another.

2.6 School Transport[5]

Local education authorities in England are required to provide transport for those of their pupils under the age of eight who live more than two miles from school and for older children who live more than three miles away. One County Authority in 1963 made transport arrangements for 36,000 children out of their school population of 245,000. The direct cost was nearly £500,000.

There are several ways of meeting the needs of school children requiring transport, the most common being:

1. By public transport, the cost being borne by the authority.
2. By buses or coaches hired for the purpose.
3. By authority-owned vehicles.

The authority whose arrangements were investigated confines itself to the first two methods, its annual expenditure on school transport being divided more or less equally between them. The Institute's study concentrated initially on the possibility of securing economies in the use of hired buses or coaches, because the problems arising under this method seemed the more susceptible to solution by operational research techniques. Three adjacent Education Divisions were selected for detailed investigation, and in these about 28 per cent of the school children had to be provided with transport.

In order to secure economy on hired transport it seemed desirable at first sight to pursue two objectives:

1. To use the seating capacity of each vehicle as fully as possible.
2. To reduce as far as possible the distance to be travelled by each vehicle.

Success in these objectives would clearly limit the number of

vehicles that needed to be hired and their running distances.
These factors do not operate independently, however, and better utilization can sometimes be achieved only at the expense
of a longer running distance. For these, and other reasons,
the design of the routes necessary to achieve the best results
is exceedingly complex. In the three Divisions that were studied, there were 14,000 children to be taken to schools. At
some of the large secondary schools, 200 children would travel
in six hired vehicles and about the same number by public
transport.

The first step in the analysis was to try to establish the
underlying factors which determined the charges made by the
transport contractors. Information was collected about the
transport requirements of the children on nearly 250 routes
and the charges being made by contractors for operating vehicles of various kinds on these routes. This information
showed wide differences in charges over various distances
traveled, as Figure 2.11 indicates.

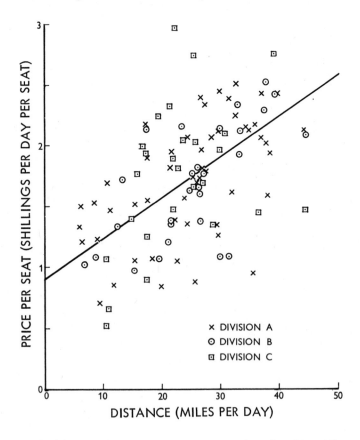

Figure 2.11. Variations in contract price for hired buses.

It will be seen that, for a route of about 25 miles per day, the price could vary between 0.8 shillings and 3 shillings for each available seat.

With the foregoing information, calculations were made using the technique of multiple regression analysis,[*] with a view to ascertaining whether any of the following factors had a particular effect on the charges being made:

1. Distance traveled.
2. The size of the vehicle on hire.
3. The age of the contract.

With the first factor, "dead" mileage was included as well as the net distance to be traveled while carrying passengers. The third factor was included because the staff concerned believed that the recent contracts were more expensive than those negotiated some years ago as a result of inflation. Eleven different calculations were made in this part of the study, but the results showed that the relationship between the contract prices and the factors chosen did not fully explain the wide differences in price.

In view of this result, it was decided to direct the next stage of the study to an identification of the other factors which might have been influencing the contract prices. Several possibilities were considered but, for various reasons, rejected. They included:

1. Class of road: it was thought that contractors might be taking traffic congestion or such factors as steepness of roads into account in settling their charges.
2. Number of pick-up points: the number of stops a vehicle had to make was also considered.

Two additional factors, however, seemed worthy of consideration, namely,

3. "Dead" mileage: the possibility of counting only a proportion of the "dead" mileage towards the total mileage was investigated. Research showed that in some cases real mileage alone was more closely related to the cost of a contract than total mileage.
4. "Monopoly" element: attempts were made to quantify the absence of local competition which it was felt had a big influence on a contractor's terms. A points system was evolved depending on the contractor's garage position in relation to those of his competitors and the relevant schools.

---

[*] Multiple regression analysis is a statistical technique used to examine the relationship between a quantity -- for example, cost -- and the elements upon which it depends. The analysis quantifies the influence of each element.

A further series of calculations was therefore carried out incorporating these factors, and making alternative assumptions for one or two of the factors used in the first analysis. Once again the result did not reveal a clear and unequivocal answer, but the following conclusions seemed to be inescapable:

1. The distances traveled and the sizes of the vehicles used had only a small effect.
2. Inflation did not have a consistent effect.
3. A monopoly situation was a consistent but not unduly important factor for most of the areas.
4. Contractors set their charges by reference to a complex set of factors which the research had so far failed to identify; or, taken together, they did so in a purely random and haphazard way.

Here then was a dilemma: Would it be worth while carrying out a detailed analysis into the routing of vehicles to try to achieve savings by reducing the mileage and improving the utilization of bus seats, while the reasons for the discrepancies between high and low prices could not be fully identified? The answer depended in part on the extent to which routes could be improved by mathematical techniques, and the ease with which the results could be put into practice. With this in mind the Institute undertook a piece of specialized mathematical research and, as a result, developed new methods by which routes could be selected. This particular analysis started from the mathematically satisfactory assumption that at each pick-up point the group of children would be taken to school by a separate vehicle. This procedure, which was feasible but inefficient, was then progressively improved in a step-by-step calculation which joined together points on the route which were in close proximity to one another and yet at a distance from the school. The exercise was continued until no reduction in the total mileage could be achieved. The mathematical techniques employed allowed the investigation to be taken a stage further with a view to reducing the seating capacity required, although at the cost of a small increase in the mileage to be run. In certain special cases, where several coaches served a group of schools, this saved one of them.

Looked at broadly, the conclusion emerged that the application of these methods to the much larger situation of the County as a whole could be expected to lead to reductions in total mileage run of approximately 5 per cent, together with reductions in the seats required of about 2 per cent. The application of the methods which had been developed would have necessitated, however, the writing of a computer program and the use of a computer, and in the situation prevailing in the authority's area

one could not be sure that realizable benefits would be secured.
Gains had to be achieved in the context of the very widely varying contract prices which were considerably influenced by un-
known factors, and route changes might cause unpredictable
price rises, for reasons which would be unidentifiable. Having
regard to these considerations, this line of action was not pursued.

The next questions considered were whether the public services were being used to the best possible extent and, conversely,
whether a transfer of children from public service to specially-
hired transport would produce savings. It was recognized that
public-service travel at season-ticket rates would often be the
cheapest form of transport. There were two situations, however, in which that would not be so. First, when a sizeable
group of children lived in the same neighborhood at a substantial distance from the school. Second, when the public-service
route used was already being traversed by a specially-hired
vehicle in which there were empty seats. In this second situation, extra children could be carried up to the capacity of the
vehicle at no extra charge, and with consequential season-ticket
savings. Detailed investigations showed that adjustments in the
second of these directions were feasible and desirable, and they
produced an annual saving of about £1,200 in the three Divisions
under investigation.

In a survey of the hired vehicles it became clear that some of
them were not being used to capacity, and the possibility of
amalgamating routes and reducing the number of hirings was
investigated. As a result of this line of inquiry, it was found
practicable to make a reduction of 6 out of some 100 hired
coaches. The savings from these rearrangements were estimated at £800 a year. In computing this figure, allowance was
made for the fact that some of the new routes would be longer
than those previously traversed, and that additional cost might
thereby be incurred on those routes.

The potential savings described in the two preceding paragraphs amount to £2,000 for the three Divisions concerned,
and would probably be equivalent to £5,000 for the County as
a whole. In addition, the staff responsible now have better
means of administering school transportation arrangements.

Looked at broadly, this study had three positive results.
First, it showed ways to possible annual savings which in the
first year should well exceed the cost of the study. Second, it
helped those administering the school-transport service to gain
a better insight into the current arrangements, and to secure a
more effective control of them. The basis of this will be the
systematic collection and analysis of information relating to
the transport of every child. Once a regular system of doing

this has been established, the administrative and financial benefits flowing from it should well outweigh any extra cost involved.

The third gain was an assessment of the value of computer
techniques in the improvement of the Authority's methods of
providing school transport. Although computers can assist in
the planning of routes to reduce distances and increase vehicle
utilization, actual savings may not be affected because of the
apparently irrational pattern of charges being made by contractors. In other words, this study revealed that the more sophis-
ticated techniques used to determine routes were of limited
value. It served as a warning against the use of such techniques,
especially when they require the use of expensive computers,
until preliminary inquiries have shown that they are likely to
produce results commensurate with the cost and effort involved.

2. 7 Conclusion

The studies described in the preceeding paragraphs have been
relatively small in scale, certainly in the amount of resources
that have been used to tackle them. For example, the work in
the South Eastern Electricity Board (see Section 2. 4) involved
two men for 18 months, and this was one of the larger problems
undertaken in the early years of the Unit's existence. The
various problems described in this Chapter may appear as tack-
ling small issues while leaving some of the major ones untouched.
In Britain, as in the United States, the growing number of cars
is having a progressively more destructive effect on the living
environment within our cities. Equally, there are complex
sociological and economic problems concerned with the size,
siting, and distribution of schools. The author takes the view
that if Operational Research is to help solve some of these big
issues, which naturally concern us all, it has first to show what
it can do and the contribution it can make in these less dramatic
fields. Then and only then will O. R. be welcomed by administrators as a valuable aid to decision making.

The experience of the Local Government Operational Research
Unit in presenting and helping British local government in the
way described has indeed led to invitations to examine some of
these big issues. Two examples may suffice to show how we
are going about this. First, in education: It is clear that whatever plans administrators may make for the development of an
education system, the more surely they can base their decisions
on good forecasts, then the better those decisions will become.
We have, therefore, made our starting point the development of
a new method of predicting how many children there will be in
various small zones of a County for periods up to ten years
ahead. A successful demonstration of how this can be done is
now working in Hertfordshire, a local education authority just

north of Greater London.[4] Similarly, with the nation's urban
traffic problems in mind, we have just begun a study which
will try to forecast people's behavior in choosing between private and public transport. This is the famous "modal split"
problem and is a key issue in the future planning of urban areas.
    Building on its early successes, the Local Government Opera-
tional Research Unit now has a staff of some 20 scientists. It
is, we hope, the beginnings of a service to British local government. It is interesting to note that local councils in Britain
spend no less than £3,600,000,000 annually.

References

1. Hartley, R., and R. A. Low, "Purchasing, Storage and
      Distribution of Domestic Appliances in a Public Board,"
      Local Government Operational Research Unit, 199 Kings
      Road, Reading, Berkshire, England.

2. Local Government Operational Research Unit, Annual
      Report 1965, L. G. O. R. U., 199 Kings Road, Reading,
      Berkshire, England.

3. Local Government Operational Research Unit, Information
      Bulletin No. 2, L. G. O. R. U., 199 Kings Road, Reading,
      Berkshire, England.

4. Local Government Operational Research Unit, New Methods
      of Forecasting Child Populations, L. G. O. R. U., 199
      Kings Road, Reading, Berkshire, England (May, 1966).

5. Ward, R. A., Operational Research in Local Government,
      George Allen and Unwin Ltd., London, 1964.

Chapter 3

SIMULATION MODELS AND URBAN PLANNING*

Harry B. Wolfe
and
Martin L. Ernst

3.1 Uses and Limitations of Models

Primary attention in this Chapter will be focused on a family
of rather broad problems which are apt to be encountered in any
effort to apply large-scale "model-making" to assist in solving
urban problems. Although reference will be made to other efforts, the main source of information will be experience acquired
during the development of a simulation model to study urban renewal in the City of San Francisco. As will become apparent,
intimate contact with this development process is necessary if
one is to describe the problems encountered without major
qualifications; however, a wide variety of informal contacts
suggests that these problems are generic generally to large-
scale model-making effort, rather than a special attribute of
the San Francisco simulation.

Background. Efforts to develop cohesive plans for improving
the housing, the industrial plant, and the aesthetic environment
of cities has a long history in almost all countries. Starting in
the 1930's, the Federal Government of the United States became
an active participant in a series of programs, which have steadily
expanded over time, concerned with halting the deterioration
of housing in our major cities. Early efforts were mostly devoted to "spot solutions" -- the direct tearing down and rebuild-
ing of specific slums -- and it is only after World War II that
significant efforts were made to treat city problems on a relatively broad base.

* Much of the material covered in this Chapter is derived from
the Arthur D. Little, Inc. Technical Paper No. 8, "Model of
San Francisco Housing Market," which was financed in part
through a Community Renewal Program Grant from the United
States Housing and Home Finance Agency under the provisions
of Section 405 of the Housing Act of 1959.

The early renewal programs tended to establish projects purely on the basis of need, as expressed by ratings of the degree of physical deterioration present in different parts of a city. Experience fairly quickly indicated that these programs were not universally successful, and that major urban deterioration was continuing at a rate at least as great as the rate at which improvements were being made. As this process continued, attention increasingly has been focused on efforts to achieve a broader and more coordinated set of mechanisms to halt deterioration, starting with the development of long-term, internally consistent plans for restoring desired urban virtues. A combination of developments -- principally the computational capacity offered by digital computers, the acquisition of increasingly complete data on urban physical and population characteristics, and the development of improved understanding of the mechanisms at work that determine land use in urban areas -- has gradually led to a number of projects on which large-scale systems analysis, or model building, has been employed in an effort to simulate the operations and interactions of a mass of variables relevant to urban planning.

The first major model of this type was developed in conjunction with the Penn-Jersey transportation study, followed by models developed for planning in Baltimore, Boston, Pittsburgh, San Francisco, and numerous other cities. Several of these models,[1] principally the Penn-Jersey and the Baltimore models, were primarily devoted to transportation planning, although the great interaction between transportation and urban development inevitably forced a high level of urban planning content into the work. Other studies, such as those for Pittsburgh and San Francisco, were oriented directly toward assisting the development of urban renewal plans and programs. The most ambitious and complex of these models, typical of the type of effort with which we are concerned here, are the Penn-Jersey, the Pittsburgh, and the San Francisco models.

These three models exhibit many differences, due to the variety of purposes for which they were developed and the environments of the urban areas under study. To illustrate the range of possible approaches:

1. The Penn-Jersey study, because of its strong transportation orientation, has stressed accessibility to opportunities of interest to urban dwellers (such as employment, shopping, etc.) as the prime factor governing the pattern of growth of urban housing; this approach implies that through planning transportation developments, the pattern of land use can be controlled to a significant degree.

2. The Pittsburgh model has emphasized employment opportunities as the prime determinant of land use; the allocation of

industry, and particularly industry dependent on specific site
characteristics, is the starting point of this effort, with land
use thereafter dependent on accessibility characteristics relative to industry location.

3. Since San Francisco is a compact, residential and commercial city rather than an industrial center, the model developed
for its study has been confined to residential housing, and is
based on establishing the "market" operations governing actions
taken to change the quantity, quality, and costs of housing available; transportation, accessibility, and similar factors are considered only indirectly.

There are many other differences among these models, but
there are also many factors which they share in common. All
are descriptive models rather than optimizing models. All
incorporate a relatively large series of sub-models, some of
which have deterministic and some of which have stochastic
characteristics. Finally, and perhaps most important for this
presentation:

1. Each has cost far more to produce than was originally
planned!

2. Each badly overran the original planned completion date!

3. Not one has yet received effective use for the purpose
which inspired their original design!

In spite of these deficiencies the authors continue to be enthu-
siastic supporters of the continued development of models of
this type. Although they have many weaknesses, they seem to
offer our best hope for understanding the impact of planned
actions on the growth and standards of quality maintained in an
urban area. Many of the weaknesses and problems encountered
should be transitory in nature. However, we must recognize
these difficulties, and take them into account in future work.

This Chapter can thus be viewed as a case history of the
problems encountered in devising a simulation model and of
the advantages and limitations of the model, once devised. The
following Section contains a discussion of the steps to be taken
in developing a model, some of the difficulties arising in taking
the steps, and some of the uses to which the model can be put,
once it is in working order. These general comments are based
on detailed experience with the San Francisco model; discussion
with other model-makers indicates that they apply, with some
changes in emphasis, to the other types of simulation models
so far developed. The next Section will outline the structure
of the San Francisco model, exemplifying the analytic and technical difficulties and how they may be overcome. The final
Section of this Chapter will contain some general conclusions
and predictions for the future.

3.2 General Considerations

The CRP Model. The mathematical computer simulation
model to be used as an example was developed by Arthur D.
Little, Inc. as part of the Community Renewal Program (CRP)
for the City and County of San Francisco.[2] The CRP itself is a
new device in urban renewal planning and programming. In
the past, local governments have typically attacked their renewal and development problems on a piecemeal, project-by-
project basis, looking at only one aspect of their overall problem at a time. As a result, traditional renewal activity has
often been inconclusive and/or inadequate, and, at times, even
divisive in dealing with the problems created by urban blight.
Through CRP, however, local governments will be able to combine many of their existing programs with some new tools and
programs, and plan them in an integrated manner on a time-
phased, priority basis. Moreover, both the public and private
sectors will be coordinated in a comprehensive, city-wide basis.
It is expected that in this way, much duplication of effort and
major program failures can be avoided.

The failures and weaknesses of renewal activity in the past
have resulted not so much from poor planning, but from the
inability of conventional methods of data analysis and forecasting to identify and measure accurately the repercussions and
consequences of various public and private actions. In other
words, it has not been possible to allow for the fact that actions
aimed at one part of the environment affect other parts, that
programs aimed at physical environment often affect the social
environment, that programs aimed at one area affect other
areas, and that planning aimed at short-term goals affects the
long-term equilibrium. Since the CRP assumes an overview
of long-range strategies for a period of twenty years and because of the integrated approach, greater impact on key problems can be achieved.

The City of San Francisco has some special problems and
characteristics. It is a small, self-contained city, and it is
possible to travel from any part of the city to any other part
within a half hour by public buses. The population of the city
is declining slightly, principally because there is a substantial
movement of middle-income families to the suburbs. The
movement of population into the city consists mainly of low-
income, mobile families. As a consequence, the nonwhite
population of the city is increasing. At present more than
20 per cent of the population of San Francisco is nonwhite.
This movement of low-income families into the city has created
a strong demand for low-cost housing. The construction of new
housing, however, is oriented towards middle-income or high-
income families. The distribution of the population by income

is now basically bimodal due to the exodus of a large number of
middle-income families to the suburbs. Regarding the state of
commerce within the city, there has been a decline in retail
business. Moreover, employment in manufacturing industries
is declining, while the demand for semiskilled and unskilled
workers is increasing. These shifts have created pressures
within the city, and unless remedial actions are taken, these
pressures are expected to increase.

In the development of the CRP model a number of general
problems arose which are present, either explicitly or implicitly,
in the devising of most urban models. They are discussed in the
next Subsections.

Selection of Appropriate Geographic Area. In our case, the
appropriate geographical unit was forced on us by the nature of
the assignment: our charter for work applied to the City of
San Francisco only, and we could not legitimately devote significant effort -- or count on necessary assistance -- in analyzing the region surrounding the city. This circumstance was in
many respects an unfortunate one, because the future of all
cities -- and even large metropolitan areas -- is strongly influenced by factors beyond their boundaries. In the case of
San Francisco, for example, it is quite clear that any substantial improvement in the quality of low-cost housing provided
within the city could immediately result in a migration from
nearby surrounding areas, which would tend toward re-estab-
lishment of an equilibrium condition throughout the entire San
Francisco Bay area. Even consideration of this area is in
some respects inadequate, since population mobility in the
United States is high, and there is what amounts to a reservoir
of inadequately housed people which appears almost infinite in
size relative to the capacity of any single metropolitan area in
the United States.

Equivalent situations undoubtedly exist in most countries.
In Italy, for example, the migration of workers from the South
to the North has been in process for many years, and the effects
of urban improvements in the North, as well as the growth
or decrease of job opportunities associated with urban development, unquestionably influence the rate of this migration.

While it is always possible to develop a model confined to a
central city, and to take care of the influence of the surrounding
areas by analyses outside the main model, this is an unsatisfy-
ing process. The selection of the desirable area for consideration should involve a compromise between size and complexity
of the resulting model -- for the level of detail appropriate to
the study purposes -- and the natural demographic and geographical structure of an area. We are not yet technically prepared to handle a whole region at the desirable level of detail

for urban planning, but a typical metropolitan area appears to
be an appropriate geographical unit.

Unfortunately, in the United States we are at a severe disad-
vantage, in that there is no political unit corresponding to a
metropolitan area. Special metropolitan area authorities can
be established for specific purposes, the most common of these
arising in connection with transportation planning, but even
here authority is in many respects limited. On many of the
most vital issues, such as housing, schools, and transportation,
our cities and their hinterlands are in conflict. Although urban
area models provide a possible means for resolving some of
these conflicts, there is little immediate hope of their use in
this manner. As a result, plans developed for the suitable
political unit (the city) are greatly weakened by what they leave
out, while plans developed for the natural social unit (the metropolitan area) simply cannot be implemented because of lack
of political cohesiveness. For the moment, we have no choice
but to live with this situation, but we must recognize it as a
source of continuing political friction and as an important barrier to the development of significant analytical techniques.

Selection of Model Philosophy. The differences of approach
that can be used in developing large models have already been
indicated. In the case of San Francisco, our philosophy was
established through consideration of the actions which it was
feasible for a city government to take. Although an appreciable
fraction of the total area of the United States is owned by the
Federal, State, and local governments, the majority of urban
area ownership is in private hands and is subject to only limited
control. A city can effect zoning laws, restricting the type of
construction which can take place in given localities; it can
exert varying degrees of building code enforcement; it can
build parks, roads, and other amenities; and it can provide
varying levels of service by major utilities. It can also,
through increased taxes, subsidize construction, rents, etc.
However, the large majority of actions affecting a city's stock
of housing will still be controlled by the activities of the many
individual owners of property. Under these conditions, it
seemed most appropriate to consider the operations of this
private market in detail. Possible activities undertaken by the
city government could then be studied in terms of their influence on the private market, in an effort to determine the extent
to which public activity can provide leverage to move the overall system in a desirable direction.

This approach was based on the particular circumstances
facing the City of San Francisco. It is obviously not the only
possible approach, and it may not be the best approach for all
cities. This implies that we probably cannot follow any single

path in the development of urban models, but must develop families of models for different purposes and circumstances. This
in turn raises problems of learning from others' experience,
borrowing techniques to reduce the cost of future efforts, and
establishing a degree of cohesiveness and continuity in the research and development of models for urban study. For the
moment we are at a point where considerable variety is necessary, and each model must be tailored to immediate needs.

Resolution of Conflicts Among Planners. Our work incorporated three significant groups of people: persons trained in city
planning, persons trained in operations research and systems
analysis, and representatives of the planning activity of the
City of San Francisco. Inevitably, conflicts developed -- primarily among the first two groups of participants. These
were largely due to the fact that teams with this mix of interests
and talents had seldom worked together previously; they required
an educational period before cohesiveness could develop. The
most severe practical problems in developing the model arose
because of the different levels of detail desired by the different
participants to support their normal pattern of work and interest.
The city planners, for example, maintained insistence on a level
of detail which bordered on impracticality, in terms of input data
requirements and output analysis. This was largely due to over-
expectation with regard to the current capabilities of simulation
techniques. The operations research personnel wished to retain
simplicity in the initial model, even at the cost of possible loss
of validity and utility of results. Experience with the use of
simulation in other fields had indicated a consistent pattern
wherein initial models were found to be over-detailed, and successive versions were almost invariably made more aggregated.
However, this process would presumably result in a model
which could not answer all questions of interest to the planners --
such as the areas of a city to which a specific population group
would move if their current dwellings were taken over for redevelopment -- although it would provide considerable data for
analyzing such problems outside the main model. The compromise finally reached probably satisfied neither party. The
level of detail incorporated led to an enormous burden of data
acquisition, processing, editing, etc. , and produced outputs at
a level of detail which led to extremely lengthy requirements
for output analysis.

The fundamental problem here is more a short-term than a
long-term one. Over a period of time there is no reason why
any desired level of detail cannot be incorporated -- provided
suitable input data can be found. But from the analytic point
of view, there are enormous gains to be achieved through
starting on a relatively simple and not too ambitious scale,

incorporating greater detail only as its potential utility is
clearly recognized. All three of the major models have suf-
fered from over-ambition in the level of detail sought in their
earliest versions, although not necessarily in the complexity
of their structure; this has been the primary source of the
unanticipated costs and time associated with their development.

Goals and Objectives. The traditional approach to urban improvement involves the establishment of goals and objectives;
these have usually been associated with the renewal of areas of
blight, and involve an assumption that such action, if pursued
vigorously, will result in continuing general improvement. We
now recognize that a city is a far more complex social organism,
with a wide mixture of inconsistent and often contradictory desires expressed by its inhabitants. The model builder is
quickly faced with the question of how the model output should
be evaluated, and what indices can be used to measure the anticipated degree of improvement. In this effort he is apt to
receive little or no help. The political authorities for whom
the work is being performed tend to be rather incoherent when
discussing this subject; most typically they talk at a level of
generality which is analytically meaningless, and one that all
too often incorporates severe internal contradictions.

Our approach to this problem was one of avoidance, and we
believe this tactic is sound both conceptually and in practice.
Our model was developed to study the implications of possible
civic actions, but did not aim to incorporate judgment as to
which of a given set of implications was most desirable. We
regard this general problem of goals and objectives as an educational problem, and one in which simulation models can play
a most important role. Once sets of implications resulting
from different feasible civic actions are made available to the
political authorities, they must be forced to make the final
evaluations; this is both their right and their responsibility.
The very process of examining the implications of feasible
civic actions and then making a selection will, in itself, assist
in the development of a rationale from which goals and objectives may eventually be defined and subjected to analysis. At
present, there are too few mechanisms for determining the
feasibility of achievement of apparently desirable objectives,
and thereby restricting those examined to a meaningful set;
this process must be the starting point, and was one toward
which our work was directed.

Objectives of the Model. In order to formulate meaningfully
a set of public actions to make effective the use of land in the
city, some questions have to be answered. In terms of residential land use, we need to consider questions such as: What
public actions can stimulate private funds into housing; what

public actions can constrain overbuilding, if such a situation
arises; what public actions favor or discriminate against supply of residential space for various types of users; what public
actions tend to cancel one another out ? The basic purpose of
the model of the housing market is to provide meaningful answers to such questions.

The unique advantage of the mathematical simulation model
is that it reproduces in an abstracted form the actual interrelationships that occur, or might occur, in the market for land
and building space in the city. The model provides an organized
structure or framework for examining relationships that exist
between the various elements that constitute the city's land and
building space market. The relationships are represented by a
set of mathematical equations. By altering the numbers and
thus affecting the relationships between certain elements, the
effect of various public or private decisions on the different
components of the city can be determined. The availability of
modern, high-speed, large-capacity electronic data-processing
computers makes feasible both the use of these techniques and
the utilization of the extensive data necessary to examine fully
the interactions of various elements of the city.

The CRP simulation model, as initially designed, deals primarily with the residential sector for which data in the detail
necessary are most available. The intent is to incorporate the
industrial and commercial sectors at a later time. The model
is intended to be an ongoing tool of the city -- to be developed,
refined, and modified in the future as conditions change.

In addition, the model should influence the city's data bank
of information on its physical and demographic characteristics.
One of the primary purposes in developing a model is to determine in more structured form the types of information necessary
to make appropriate and good decisions concerning civic policy.
As one of its by-products, the model would result in the development of a bank of data on the city and its inhabitants that is relatively unique and would not be developed otherwise. These data
are developed because of the model's need for quantitative information about the important elements of the urban system. Thus,
the model serves to screen out from the vast amount of potential
urban data that which is most significant.

The simulation model has been developed to achieve several
purposes:

1. To develop alternative, long-range strategies and programs for renewal and development of the city, and to
   indicate the costs and benefits of each strategy and
   program.
2. To serve as an ongoing tool of the city government, to
   permit the city officials to have available on a continuing

basis a method for testing the consequences of various
renewal actions before they have actually taken place.
3. To identify key statistical symptomatic indicators which
should be maintained on a continuing basis so that the
city can be aware of the rate and direction of changes
affecting it and take appropriate responsive action.
4. To improve the flow of information and utilize more
effectively and in greater detail the available information.

Limitations of the Model. It should be borne in mind at the
outset that the model is not a "black box" that can take a set of
input values and convert these into a specific plan for action by
the city authorities. If a specific plan is fed into the model,
the model cannot even determine whether or not this is the best
possible plan for a given set of circumstances. The model is,
however, a tool to assist experienced planners in evaluating
results that might be achieved through following a given course
of action. It is not a substitute for experience and judgment,
but it is a means for permitting these qualities to be focused
more effectively on the areas that need greatest attention.
Since human desires and interests are highly diverse, machines
or models with their attendant rigidity cannot be expected to
solve a problem involving a variety of vital human inputs. A
city is far too complex an organism to be completely subject to
mechanistic analysis. A model can at best give a starting point
and improve the efficiency with which human analysts and planners can operate.

Checks on Accuracy. The long-term predictive accuracy of
the model can be checked only after several years. The model
was designed to employ 1960 census data as input; these provide the best and most reliable source of information on many
characteristics of the population of San Francisco. Theoreti-
cally, the accuracy of the model could be studied by starting
the model in 1950 and seeing whether its results duplicated the
actual events of the later years. Unfortunately, the detailed
data from the 1950 census that might have been used for cali-
bration and testing purposes are not available in a form permitting the necessary cross-tabulations. The model was therefore
calibrated to the construction activity in San Francisco during
the period 1960-1964 by an extensive series of tuning runs.

In general, the model is not expected to be a highly accurate
tool for forecasting the total future investment to improve
housing in the City of San Francisco. There are a variety of
reasons for this, ranging from technical problems associated
with the development of input data to the intent involved in developing the model. The level of building in a city such as San
Francisco depends not only on general economic conditions in
the Bay area, but also on psychological attitudes toward the

construction of major new building units and the influences of
competitive factors on potential investors both in the city and
in the surrounding areas. In the development of the model no
particular emphasis was placed either on forecasting general
economic conditions or on trying to cope with the psychological
problems that influence large-scale building. Rather than
being concerned with estimates of the absolute building level,
the model is primarily intended to develop an understanding of
how the total building effort would be divided among competing
possible forms of land usage, and how the residents of the city
would be influenced by this division.

The results of using the model must be adopted as suggestions
rather than as directions or proofs. The results will "suggest"
that if certain actions are taken, certain events will occur.
These events should not be accepted as proved, but should be
evaluated in terms of experience and judgment. In some cases,
the validity of the model results will be immediately clear and
hence accepted. In other cases, it will be necessary to examine
the analysis in considerable detail to determine why the results
occurred. This process of determining the "why" of a set of
results can often add substantially to knowledge of the factors
that influence a city's pattern of growth. In some cases, the
logical explanations of why the model produced certain results
will not be entirely acceptable as representing the real world,
and in these cases the results must be rejected.

Degree of Complexity. The original version of the model is
not easy to employ. It involves a relatively complex computer
program of some 30,000 to 35,000 individual computer instruc-
tions. Between 12,000 and 15,000 items of input data must be
employed on each run. The large majority of these input data
will not change from one run to the next, so they can be used
repeatedly. Nevertheless, for any new run devoted to the study
of a new situation, it will be necessary to incorporate some new
input data and, under some conditions, some new computer in-
structions. Interpretation of the results of the model is also
quite demanding. The outputs are of a form requiring skill to
disaggregate and develop suitable tables, and the interpretation
thereafter must be done by people who are not only acquainted
with details of the model but who are also thoroughly experienced
with the City of San Francisco and with the characteristics of
its housing and construction activities.

It is evident now that the level of detail in the current model
is greater than is necessary, and that removal of some of this
detail would make it far easier and less expensive to operate
and employ. Furthermore, fundamental improvements should
be incorporated in a number of areas. Typical of these is the
development of more "feedback loops" in the model, such as

the influence of public housing expenditures on the tax rate and
thence on movements of residents into and out of the city. Finally, as we have gained experience in analyzing the model outputs, we have determined ways in which the form of the outputs
could be improved to make them more easily utilized. The
utility of the model can thus be improved through incorporating
changes in the data input and output and through additions to the
internal structure of the model itself. We are currently assisting the City Planning Department in making some of these
changes to the program.

Role of Operations Research. The term "Operations Research"
is often loosely used, but it has been made a little precise in the
past decade through its actual practice in various fields. According to Morse,[3] operations research is "the scientific study of
operations," where "an operation is a pattern of activity of men,
or of men and machines, engaged in carrying out a cooperative
and usually repetitive task, with (specified) goals and according
to specified rules of operation. .... Its object is to understand
the behavior of various operations, by the appropriate use of
observation(s), controlled experimentation and theoretical analysis, so as to predict the operational result of changes in operating rules, and thus better to control the operation and improve
its result."

The CRP is principally a decision-making process -- an attempt to obtain the "most" with limited resources. Business
firms may have a comparatively clear-cut notion of what they
mean by the "most," but in the case of urban planning, the concept is ill defined. One of the basic purposes of this model is
to assist in establishing the criteria of choice. In matters of
urban planning, the test of preferred choice is more implicit
than explicit, more intuitive than rational. In developing the
model, however, the criteria are made more explicit. Moreover, in problems of choice, one of the primary requirements
is to consider the consequences of alternative policies. The
model of the real situation was developed to assist in predicting
the consequences of alternative public actions.

The role of operations research in the public sector is probably more vital than in the private sector. A model based on
the real situation serves as a continuous feedback process in
the analysis and evaluation of the operation of decision-making
in the complex domain of an aggregate of human beings. In the
light of existing criteria, different alternatives are evaluated
and this, in turn, leads to a further refinement of the criteria.
In view of the intrinsic variability in human behavior, this process must be dynamic. The complexity of the problem and the
necessarily adaptive character of the actions can best be achieved
through an integrated, interdisciplinary operations research type
of study.

3.3 Model Structure

The CRP model is primarily concerned with predicting the
effect of alternative public actions on the city's housing stock.
The model is, in effect, a replication of the land and building
space market in San Francisco. It simulates those factors of
the urban system that determine housing unit quality, quantity,
location, price, and type within a geographical area.

Model Operation. Market structure generalizations from
economics were used to construct the model. Additional hypothesis testing and development were required, however, to
select operating characteristics as rules for the decision-making
variables or elements replicated within the model. These operating characteristics are symbolically expressed to replicate the
behavioral and economic motivations of the decision makers who
interact in the "real world" housing market. The reliability of
the model is largely dependent on the accuracy of these rules or
postulates. In addition to decision-making elements, the model
includes elements that represent the housing stock in the 1960
census. Model outputs are detailed predictions of the state of
the housing stock at various time periods.

Outputs are generated by simulating an equilibrium-seeking
system that is never allowed to reach equilibrium. Certain
basic components of this system are altered by the exogenous
insertion of altered population figures at regular intervals.
Exogenous constraints on the actions of decision-making elements can also be inserted at intervals to simulate restriction-
type public actions.

Households are allocated by the model at periodic intervals.
The model is programmed to simulate the adjustment of the
housing market to pressures generated by these allocations in
view of institutional and governmental constraints. Household
allocations, although recorded in the computer print-out, are
not the desired final output. They alter the rents for each of
the locational, type, and quality housing categories monitored
by the model. The rent changes then react with construction
costs, rehabilitation costs, and physical aging rates to alter
the housing inventory.

The operation of the model is based on matching, in the computer, existing stocks of housing with potential "users." Changes
in the amount or quality of housing occur when the users of space,
because of an increase in their number or an increase in their
ability to pay, create a "pressure" for certain types of housing.
In time, a high pressure causes rents to rise. Changes in the
housing stock are generated within the computer to relieve this
pressure if the change or "transition" is financially feasible.
Financial feasibility is determined by comparing the cost of
making the change with the anticipated future yield. If this

comparison indicates that profitable development conditions
exist, the computer adds an appropriate number of new dwelling
units to the inventory of the city's housing stock; makes a notation of the transition cost in a summary of total construction
investment; and subtracts a number of older units from the inventory to account for the demolition necessary to make room
for the new units. The computer then computes the resulting
shifts in pressures, rent levels, and vacancy rates. When all
effects have been accounted for, new inputs are fed in and the
process repeats. In this way, over a series of iteration periods,
a new configuration of housing usage is generated, simulating
the physical development of the city's housing market. This
process is repeated for nine 2-year periods, providing an 18-
year forecast in a complete run.

Public-action programs and policies are introduced into the
simulation as they affect the operation of the market, either by
interfering with, influencing, or controlling its functioning.
Such actions take the form of zoning ordinances prohibiting
certain changes in the use of space; code enforcement and renewal projects "artifically" introducing changes in space use
where profitable development conditions may not exist; financial measures, such as cost subsidies or mortgage guarantees;
and public improvements that can alter the relative attractive-
ness of neighborhoods and thus affect the demand for housing.
The resultant effect of the alternative public-action programs
and policies on the allocation of housing usage may be evaluated
in terms of the city's goals and objectives.

In summary, then, the model simulates the interactions and
effects on residential housing of (1) public policies, programs,
and actions; (2) investment behavior of the private market; and
(3) the location decisions of households. The interrelationship
of the model with the environment is shown very simply in
Figure 3.1.

Model Elements. The elements of the model may be classified as follows:

1. Housing Stocks

   a. Neighborhoods. San Francisco was divided into 106
"neighborhoods" (Figure 3.2). Each neighborhood is approximately the size of a census tract, although neighborhood boundaries are not necessarily the boundaries of census tracts.
The neighborhood is the smallest geographic area that can be
identified in the simulation run. A redevelopment project, code
enforcement, or a new high-rise apartment building can be
placed in a given neighborhood, but its position within the neighborhood is not stated in the model. Neighborhoods were chosen
to represent as closely as possible areas with similar amenities,
qualities of housing, or predominant housing types.

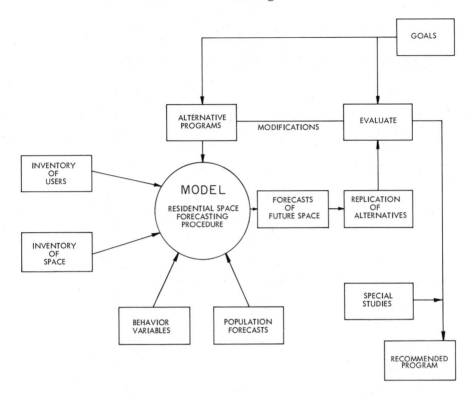

Figure 3.1. Interrelationship of the model with the environment.

  b. Location Categories. Each neighborhood was assigned
a "location number" depending on amenities and other factors
distinguishing the area. The fourteen location categories were
set up according to Table 3.1.

  c. Fracts. The fundamental unit of housing in the computer
is the dwelling unit. In order to keep the inventory of space in
the city within the memory capacity of a large computer, we
invented for model purposes a land unit that we call a "fract."
In current model runs, a fract is equal to two acres. There
are 4,980 fracts of residential land in the city (including vacant
land available for residential development). Each fract is homo-
geneous with respect to its space type and condition; a fract
cannot have mixed land use within it. A fract lies within the
boundaries of its neighborhood and represents a grouping of
parcels in different parts of a neighborhood having a common
housing type and condition. Transitions in use of space and
housing (new construction, or changes in condition of the stock)
occur a complete fract at a time.

  d. Land-Use Type: J Types. Dwelling units are divided
among 24 categories characterized by tenure, number of rooms,

Table 3. 1. Location Category Definitions

L	Topography	Modal Structure Type	Range of Mean Monthly Rent
1	Hilly	SF	$0-140
2	Hilly	SF	140-275
3	Hilly	SF	275+
4	Hilly	5+	$0-75
5	Hilly	5+	75-115
6	Hilly	5+	115+
7	Level	SF	$0-125
8	Level	SF	125-175
9	Level	SF	175+
10	Level	2-4	$0-75
11	Level	2-4	75+
12	Level	5+	$0-75
13	Level	5+	75-115
14	Level	5+	115+

Table 3.2. List of J Housing Types

J	Structure	Tenure	Rooms
2	Single Family	Rent	1-2
3	Single Family	Own	1-4
4	Single Family	Rent	3-4
5	Single Family	Own	5-6
6	Single Family	Rent	5-6
7	Single Family	Own	7+
8	Single Family	Rent	7+
9	Public Structures		
10	Vacant Land		
12	2-4	Rent	1
14	2-4	Rent	2
15	2-4	Own	1-4
16	2-4	Rent	3-4
17	2-4	Own	5-6
18	2-4	Rent	5-6
19	2-4	Own	7+
20	2-4	Rent	7+
22	5+	Rent	1
24	5+	Rent	2
25	5+	Public Housing	3-4
26	5+	Rent	3-4
27	5+	Public Housing	5+
28	5+	Rent	5-6
30	5+	Rent	7+

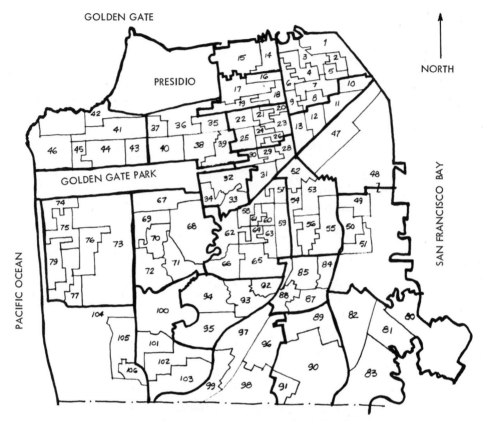

Figure 3.2. San Francisco "neighborhood" divisions.

and structure type. Table 3.2 shows the number (J type) assigned to each dwelling unit type. Not all dwelling unit types
are represented in every location category. For instance,
there are very few owner-occupied single-family units in L-4
neighborhoods.

e. Condition. The J number, location category, and condition of a dwelling unit are sufficient to specify the kind of
housing in the model. We divided housing into four conditions,
as shown in Table 3.3.

Table 3.3. Condition Categories

Condition 1	Sound
Condition 2	Needs minor repairs
Condition 3	Deteriorating
Condition 4	Dilapidated

The condition categories are used in six different ways:

1. People perceive differences in the quality of housing and

react. Those who can afford high rentals will normally
look first for Condition 1, with Condition 2 as a possible
alternative. Those who can afford only minimal rents
will avoid Condition 1 and normally look for more space
per dollar, or lower-condition housing.

2. Dwelling units in better condition normally command a
higher rental than those in worse condition.

3. Conditions 3 and 4 are generally considered substandard
dwelling units and are subject to a code enforcement program, if instituted in the appropriate neighborhood. When
code enforcement is applied to a Condition 3 or Condition 4
dwelling unit, it must be raised to Condition 1 during the
succeeding period.

4. Housing deteriorates in time to a lower condition state.

5. If two properties are currently realizing the same rental
income, the property in better condition will command
the higher market value, based on its probable future
income. This effect is achieved by imposing the condition
that "normal yield" for a lower-condition unit is generally
greater than for a higher-condition unit. This is used primarily in the formula:

$$\text{Market value} = \frac{\text{Current Rental}}{\text{Normal Yield}}$$

6. The cost of rehabilitating is higher for a unit with a larger
condition number.

2. Space Transitions

   a. Public Actions. Public actions may affect housing directly, restrict the options of private developments, or tend
to encourage the kind of desired action. The model can simulate the following public actions:

   i. Zoning: Two zoning numbers can be entered for
      each neighborhood. The first number is the maxi-
      mum number of fracts that can be built with large
      apartments, that is, a building with 5+ dwelling
      units (J types 21 or above). If a large apartment
      house is being considered for this area, the compu-
      ter first checks whether there are already the maxi-
      mum number of 5+ fracts already in the neighborhood.
      The second zoning restriction number in the building
      table is the maximum numbers of fracts with build-
      ings of two or more dwelling units (J types 11 or
      above). A change of zoning policy may be simulated
      by changing these zoning restriction numbers.

   ii. Location Table: It is possible to simulate a change
       in the amenities of any given neighborhood by chang-
       ing its location category. In this case, the demand

picture for housing in this neighborhood would be
changed. An example of how this could occur would
be if the city were to change the amenities of a given
neighborhood, perhaps by building a park.

iii. Assessment: A change in the assessment rate, or
any other factor affecting the normal yield, can be
simulated by changing the normal yield of a given
JcL housing type (combination of J type, c condition,
and L location category).

iv. Rental: The rental value for a given JcL can be
changed externally.

v. Capital Improvement: Any fract can be designated
for a capital improvement and "J type 9" can be
built on that fract. J type 9 represents public property not usable for residential purpose, such as
fire stations, parks, libraries, etc.

vi. Binary Flags: There are six binary "flags" that can
be turned ON or OFF for each fract in the city.
These are handled in the following manner:

We assume that two projects will not occur on the
same property within a two-year cycle period. Thus,
when a transition has occurred on a given fract the
computer turns one flag ON, signifying that this
fract is not available for another transition in the
same period. Flags on all fracts are turned OFF at
the beginning of the next time period.

A different flag is used to signify that a given fract
is owned by a public agency until this flag is turned
OFF exogenously.

A third flag indicates whether or not a fract is available for occupancy, in spite of its ownership by a
public body. In other words, the city may purchase
property for a redevelopment project and allow households to continue to occupy the housing for a few
years.

A fourth flag signifies a fract on which code enforcement has been applied. If this flag is ON, and the
property is in substandard condition, some transition,
even if uneconomic, must occur during this time cycle
to bring the property up to code. The computer
chooses the transition with the highest yield.

The last two flags are used to designate fracts in a
rehabilitation or a redevelopment area. The transition cost is reduced (by 10 per cent for a rehabilitation area and by 20 per cent for a redevelopment
area), simulating the kind of financial aid the city
would normally offer.

vii. Code Enforcement: Code enforcement may be applied to a given percentage of units in designated neighborhoods. The computer chooses a random number for each substandard fract; if the random number shows that this fract has code enforcement applied against it, then the code enforcement flag is turned ON.

viii. Construction Costs: Aid for construction of certain J types can be simulated by reducing the construction costs of a given transition.

b. Private Market Transitions.

i. Yield and Rent: Although public actions represent one mechanism by which transitions are brought about in space types and land use, the more important mechanism of transition in the simulation model is that associated with the "yield ratio," representing decisions by private developers.

With each JcL type of property are associated two parameter values, rental and normal yield. The initial rental values are the average rents for each JcL type of property, obtained from a special analysis of the 1960 census data. The normal yield is defined as:

$$\text{Normal Yield (JcL)} = \frac{\text{Rental (JcL)}}{\text{Market Value (JcL)}}$$

In addition to net return on investment, the yield figure must include normal or average out-of-pocket expenses, such as the interest rate, provision for risk, other financing rates, normal expected vacancy rate, taxes and insurance rates, upkeep, maintenance, and management expenses.

The rules adopted in this simulation for the execution of private market transitions or projects are as follows:

1. A transition represents the change of one fract to a different J type or a different condition.

2. A transition will be executed whenever the yield for this transition is equal to or greater than the normal yield for the type of space resulting from the project, provided no external constraints forbid it.

If the transition involves rehabilitation, conversion, or merger, the yield formula depends upon the increased rental:

$$\text{Transition yield} = \frac{\text{Rent (New Condition) - Rent (Old Condition)}}{\text{Cost}_J \text{ (Old to New Condition)}}$$

For the building of a new structure, however, yield
depends on the total rental to be realized from the
new structure and the cost of the project, including
both the building costs and the market value of the
property in its old state:

$$\text{Transition yield} = \frac{\text{Rent (New JcL)}}{\text{Cost}_{\text{JcL}}\text{(New Construction)} + \text{Market Value (Old JcL)}}$$

The yield ratio is defined as:

$$\text{Yield ratio} = \frac{\text{Transition Yield}}{\text{Normal Yield (JcL)}}$$

Yield ratio must be greater than unity for a transition to be executed by the private market.

Total construction and rehabilitation transition costs
are cumulated so that at the end of a simulation run
we have estimates of the total private market investment by period, for an 18-year period.

ii. Space Pressure:

   a) Pressure: Space pressure is computed as the
   ratio between the demand for a housing type and
   the supply. Demand is computed as the sum of
   the "relevant households," where a relevant household is one that would normally seek this type of
   property, and could afford to pay the rent if it
   were vacant.

   b) Rent Computation: During each cycle of each period
   the model recomputes the rental value for every
   JcL in the model. This computation makes use of
   a value-of-space pressure according to the graph
   in Figure 3.3. The graph was developed on the
   basis of data on San Francisco vacancy rates and
   rents, and on the empirical work of Black and
   Winnick in other cities.[4]

   The meaning of the graph is as follows: If the
   pressure is well above 1, indicating that a larger
   number of households desire the particular housing
   type than there is stock available, then rents are
   caused to increase at a maximum rate. If the
   pressure is well below 1, there would be a strong
   incentive for owners to reduce rents in order to
   increase the occupancy rate of their property. If
   pressures are slightly lower than 1, the situation
   is ambiguous. Rather than reduce the rent for the
   units that are currently occupied, the owner may
   gain more by tolerating a slight vacancy. Further-

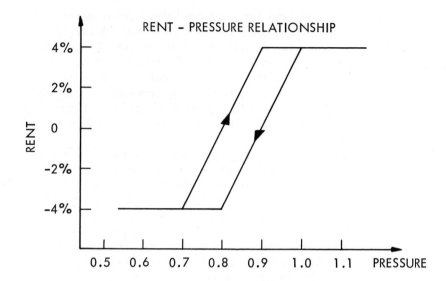

Figure 3.3. Rent-pressure relationship.

more, if the pressure is increasing with time,
landlords will assume a basically more optimistic
outlook than if the pressure is decreasing.   Thus,
one curve is used for rising pressure and the
other curve is used if pressure is decreasing.
We thus have a rent-pressure "hysteresis" effect.
No matter how high the pressure is, rents do not
increase faster than 4 per cent a year. We assume a similar maximum decreasing rate for low
pressure.

c) Households: To identify groups of households that
have similar housing needs, locational preferences,
and housing budgets, we divided the population into
114 household types, using the following attributes:
i) Household Type
(a) No children, head under 60 years.
(b) No children, head over 60 years.
(c) Households with children.
ii) Household Size: (1, 2, 3+), (1-2, 3-4, 5+), or
(1, 2, ...) depending on type and race.
iii) Race
(a) White.
(b) Negro.
(c) Oriental and others.
iv) Annual Income: The set of divisions depends on
type and color.
d) Rent-Paying Ability: We developed rent-paying

distributions for each household type, based on
actual rents paid in 1960. For most household
groups, the distribution follows closely a Gaus-
sian or "normal" probability curve, which we
truncated at the top and bottom 10 per cent of
each household group. The rent-paying distributions of household groups with the very highest or
very lowest incomes are skewed toward the upper
tail.

e) Household Preference Lists: We developed raw
counts for the number of each household type in
each housing type from the Bureau of the Census
data on a 20 per cent sample of all households in
the City of San Francisco. We normalized the
raw counts according to the total number of each
household type in the sample and the number of
housing units of each JcL type, to come up with
an index of preference.

c. Generalized Aging Model. There are three directions
in which housing condition may change. The decisions regarding the amount of money that will be expended on the maintenance, remodeling, and building of dwelling units determine the
directional impact of the aging process upon the condition of
the dwelling units in the housing inventory.

i. Rehabilitation: If the costs of improving the condition of a dwelling unit are exceeded by the extra
rents users will pay because of the condition improvement, the suppliers of these dwelling units will
increase their net income by expending the funds
necessary to improve the condition of the structures.
If the opportunity for rental increases is greater
than the total cost of constructing a new building,
including the cost of razing, then the existing structure can profitably be torn down and a new structure
will replace it.

ii. Accelerated Aging: If the money saved by cutting
back on maintenance (and thereby allowing conditions
to deteriorate) exceeds the loss of revenue that accom-
panies such downward conditional changes, then suppliers can gain in net income by allowing existing
conditions to deteriorate. The standard units soon
become substandard. We call this process "accelerated aging."

iii. Normal Aging: If neither of the above two processes
are desirable from the economic standpoint of the
landlord, he will attempt to maintain the existing
condition of his buildings with a minimum of

expenditure. In this case we have "normal aging or deterioration;" the rate of deterioration or obsolescence depends on the degree of usage, the kind of structure, and the neighborhood.

Owners of housing in a given neighborhood will tend to maintain their housing uniformly. Housing users attach value to location, and the opportunities facing landlords will tend to be uniform in a given neighborhood as user alternatives are restricted to locationally linked alternatives. In addition, the houses of a neighborhood tend to be alike in capital value.

The normal aging is assumed to be a first-order Markov process. An "aging vector" is applied against the state of housing of each type and locational category. The housing state is the number of units in conditions 1, 2, 3, 4 (and in vacant land). The elements of the aging vector represent the fraction of units that deteriorate each two-year period from a given condition to the next lower condition. The numerical values of these aging vectors were developed from a cross-sectional analysis of data on the number and condition of housing types in San Francisco, obtained in the 1960 census. A random number is generated for each fract to control the aging process. (This and code enforcement represent the only two areas in the simulation model where stochastic processes are employed.)

The accelerated aging vector generally represents a rate of deterioration approximately 10 per cent per year higher than the normal rates.

Model Flow Chart. Figure 3.4 represents a very abbreviated flow chart of the computer simulation model. A complete run will normally consist of nine complete periods, each period representing two years. Some comments on the individual steps in Figure 3.4 follow:

Step 1. All the initializing data for the run are entered into the computer, including current housing data, yield data, household preference lists, etc.

Step 2. For each time period, the housing stock is "aged," utilizing the aging vectors described under Generalized Aging Model.

Step 3. The target or forecast population and the public actions programmed for the period are entered.

Step 4. The public actions are executed.

Step 5. An allocation of households to housing fracts is carried out, utilizing the household preference lists, and availabilities and rents for each housing type are then calculated.

Step 6. A list of likely private market transitions is developed

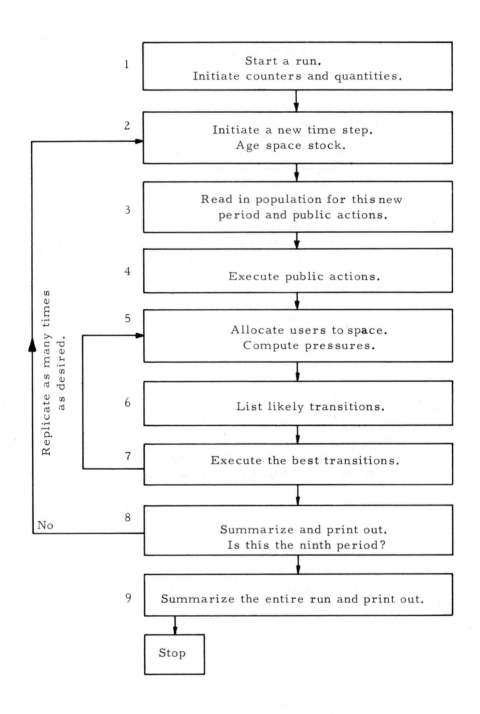

Figure 3.4. Abbreviated flow chart.

in the following manner:

    a. Determine the housing type with the highest pressure. Search throughout the city for, first, a neighborhood zoned for this kind of space and, second, a fract within this neighborhood that can be transformed to the housing type in demand.

    b. Compute a yield for this project, based on rent for the housing type in demand, the rent of the current space, and the transition cost.

    Of the transitions for which the yield is greater than the normal yield, the computer identifies those with the highest yield and puts these into a list of potential transitions. Then a list of potential transitions is built up by identifying the space type with the second-highest pressure, third-highest pressure, and so forth, until a specified maximum number of potential transitions is developed.

Step 7. The potential transitions are executed in order of yield so long as the transition is allowed by zoning restrictions, and the fract has not already undergone a transition in the period.

    The model is programmed to perform any desired number of Allocate/ List Transitions/ Execute iterations (Steps 5, 6, 7) per two-year time cycle.

Step 8. Such statistics as the detailed state of the housing, the household allocation, pressures, and rents for the period are printed out.

    Steps 2-8 are then repeated until the total number of desired periods has been simulated.

Step 9. The results of the entire run are put on an output tape for special summary tabulations and print-outs.

The CRP simulation model of the residential housing market in San Francisco is operational, and has been turned over to the City Planning Department. Most of the computer program was written in FORTRAN IV, while certain subprograms were written in assembly language. Execution of the total program takes approximately $2\frac{1}{2}$ hours of IBM 7094 computer time. A 1301 disc file was used on line.

    Extension of the CRP Simulation Model. The present model may be extended as follows:

1. Reprogramming of the Present Model

    a. Reduction of Detail. As mentioned earlier, it has become evident that the level of detail in the current model should be reduced for ease and economy of operation.

    b. Output Summary. The output summary should be reprogrammed to provide the most commonly required information in more convenient form.

2. Extending the Present Model

a. <u>Endogenous Locational Changes.</u> The factors that determine the locational category of a given neighborhood may change
cufficiently over the period of the simulation run that the neighborhood will change from one locational category to another. A
subprogram could be written that will monitor these factors and
automatically change the locational category of a neighborhood
when appropriate.

b. <u>Population Feedback Loops.</u> At present, the population
projections are input to the computer model as exogenous variables. If research can determine the relationship between population and the housing variables, then these relationships can be
incorporated into the model as "feedback loops."

c. <u>Extension of Public Actions.</u> We have programmed into
the model the important public actions that directly affect the
condition or availability of housing stock. If the effect of public
actions that indirectly affect the housing stock can be quantified,
then these public actions can be incorporated in the model.

d. <u>Monitoring and Confirmation of Housing Preferences.</u>
The preferences currently in the model were drawn from the
empirical evidence available in the 1960 census cross-tabulation.
However, housing-demand preferences may change over a
period of time; these changes should be reflected in the model
program.

e. <u>Capital Availability.</u> No test of capital availability was
made in the model. This would be an important factor in determining the growth of the housing stock.

3. <u>Expanded Simulation Model.</u> The following represent areas
where the present simulation model can serve as the basis for
the development of a model with greater scope:

a. <u>Inclusion of Industrial and Commercial Sectors.</u> Exten-
sion of the residential model to include the commercial and
industrial building stock will allow the interactions and competition for land to be studied, and the impact of public actions on
any of the three sectors to be determined.

b. <u>Regional Model.</u> The present model can serve as a
basis for an extended regional model. In such a model it
would of course be necessary to make modifications in the
scope and detail of the individual elements, to fit it within the
framework of a regional model. It would very likely be necessary to make the role of transportation availability and commut-
ing more explicit as well as to consider the general population
movement patterns.

<u>Continuity in Research and Application.</u> The San Francisco
model is now available and operating; later discussion will
indicate some of the events that have resulted from its existence.
Before doing so, however, it is important to describe some of

the problems which affect the long-term development of this
type of model. The first of these is the difficulty of establishing continuity in research and application. There have been
noted previously several of the factors which led to the necessity of confining the present model to the City of San Francisco
and of tailoring it for that city's environment. This has been
characteristic of most of the large models developed in the
United States. At the present time, there is no easy mechanism
for extending, improving, and broadening the applicability of
these models. The need to serve a specific client with limited
resources inhibits building sufficient generality into the models
at the time they are constructed. As a result, we are developing a library of computer programs built at great expense but
with limited potential usage.

The difficulty here again tends to be a political one. Applied
urban research involving large functioning models generally
cannot be performed by our main source of basic research --
the universities -- since continuing intimate contact with the
practical and political problems of individual cities is a necessary input if practical results are to be achieved. Up to the
present time, we do not have a source of support for the rather
broad-scale development and application of generalized models
useful for many cities. The recent establishment of the Department of Housing and Urban Development may provide the necessary mechanism, but until such a broad program is established
there appears to be an enormous amount of duplication, overlap,
and inefficiency inherent in the process we are forced to follow.

Costs of Application. Closely related to the previous topic is
the problem of the costs of applying and using the model. The
development and updating of the input data has already been
indicated as being an extremely expensive process. Computer
time in itself is not unduly costly, but the careful analysis of
results to ensure proper interpretation of results is time-
consuming and requires a high level of skill. The barrier here
again is a temporary one, involving the education of city planning personnel in the use of large-scale models. As will be
described shortly, however, there is an important pay-off in
the process, since the skills developed in using the model have
been found valuable in many other planning functions.

3.4 Prospects for the Future

Some of the previous discussion, particularly that of the last
Subsection, may seem pessimistic in attitude. In spite of the
difficulties mentioned, however, the authors of this Chapter
are quite optimistic in regard to the future of simulation models
for urban planning. This final Section mentions some of the
reasons for this optimism.

Uses of the San Francisco Model. Originally we hoped to
have the San Francisco simulation model available in time to
assist in the development and selection of specific urban renewal plans and programs which were to be provided to the city
authorities. Unfortunately we were not able to complete our
work in time, so the model made no major contribution to the
planning process itself. It did, however, serve to verify to a
large extent -- but not completely -- the plans which of necessity had been prepared by more conventional means. In this
manner, therefore, the San Francisco model failed to meet the
purposes for which it was designed. However, it was completed
and calibrated, has been operated successfully, and is now available and in limited use.

Although the model failed to fulfill our original plans for its
use, in the long run it has a good chance of being highly successful. Here are the reasons for this belief:

1. The San Francisco simulation has been a particularly
fruitful model. On every computer run that has been conducted --
even those which had major errors in the input data -- something of significance has been learned. For example, when the
input data on the size of an important population group were set
too high by a factor of ten, the model essentially gave a response
to the question: "If this population group was increased in size
by a factor of ten, how would this influence the supply and characteristics of housing available in the City of San Francisco
and the degree to which housing demand was filled?" In a
sense, therefore, every run has provided the answer to some
hypothetical question. Sometimes the questions had a degree
of practical interest while in other cases they were relatively
unrealistic. However, the analysis of these runs, even when
concerned with unrealistic questions, inevitably taught the
analyst something more about the structure of the City of San
Francisco and the economic relationships which govern housing
availability in that city.

2. The model has been a particularly exciting one. On almost every run, the major portion of output results indicate
housing characteristics and availability much in line with what
an experienced city planner would expect. However, in each
run there are apt to be certain "surprising" results. Most of
these can be explained rapidly, almost by inspection -- one
looks and says "I never thought about it that way, but the result
does make sense." A smaller fraction of these surprises take
rather elaborate tracing of the logical relationships to determine the interactions which were responsible. This process
in itself is both educational and rewarding, and in almost all
cases the explanation for the unusual results contributed significantly to an understanding of the processes at work.

The potential of the model also has exciting implications for the future. For many years there has been debate concerning a variety of relatively radical possibilities for improving either the housing or economic position of those inadequately housed. The model furnishes at least a starting point for testing these possibilities, and will begin to take discussion on these matters out of the realm of rhetoric and down to a level where there are numbers and concepts sufficiently solid to be criticized and analyzed in a valid way.

3. The model has had enormous educational impact. The first evidence of this impact was on the participants in its development themselves. For example, the young junior planner assigned by the City of San Francisco to the project acquired a level of knowledge and understanding of the operation of the city which has led to his receiving a promotion and rapid growth in status. In fact, although he is still responsible for liaison with regard to the model, he has become very difficult to talk to -- simply because the knowledge he has acquired has made him almost invaluable for handling a host of matters in other areas which are the concern of the City Planning Department. His participation in the model has greatly improved his status in a valid way -- by providing him a unique experience and fund of knowledge which has wide-spread utility.

4. Finally, the model is a "used" model. We cannot yet say for sure that it will be a "useful" model for the planning activity, but all evidence suggests that this will be the case. The city officials of San Francisco have been sufficiently intrigued by the preliminary results achieved and by the many possibilities for broader application in the future, that their current annual budget has provided funds for model improvements and for further operation and application. The funding is not large, but it is sufficient to ensure that the model will receive continuing attention and use. We have every hope that if this use proves successful in meeting day-to-day needs, the budgetary support will be continued and the city will have acquired a working tool which is useful for a variety of purposes.

Final Comments. Let us then summarize briefly our position with respect to the use of large models in urban planning. First, we can state that at least qualified success in their development and application has been achieved. We do not yet have a good validation of these models, in the sense of a demonstration that they give correct answers to specific questions, nor do we yet have adequate evidence that they will receive steady employment once they have been developed. However, the impact of these models has been sufficient during their short operating life and the results achieved have been sufficiently exciting, that there is no question but that they do have a future as a planning tool.

We might not be able to take this position so strongly if we had available alternate means which showed equal or greater potential for successful growth. However, metropolitan area problems are growing rapidly, while the older and traditional tools have proven steadily less satisfying. They càn still be effective in the hands of skilled practitioners, but skilled practitioners are always scarce. In the absence of an adequate supply of these traditional skills or of other better alternatives, the models will have an increasingly important role to play.

It is obvious that we have a number of important problems to solve before the models can have wide-spread application; some of the more significant ones have been discussed in this Chapter. Most of the problems are capable of solution, and our experience has indicated some of the paths which should be followed. The practical rules one should seek to follow in further development should include at least the following:

1. All initial efforts should seek to utilize a relatively simple model. Such complexity as is established should be in the structural relationships contained within the model, rather than in the data base which is being employed to operate it.

2. Whenever time or funding imposes severe limits, fairly rigid and careful plans should be employed to ensure that a working model is available when no more than two thirds of the time and budget have been spent. If this rule cannot be enforced, one will find that inadequate resources are available to test and use the model properly.

3. The model must be developed with a clear understanding of the political possibilities and limitations that will be imposed by its users. Too much effort in the United States has probably been devoted to the development of plans that are politically and socially unfeasible and unacceptable. Proper development of large models implies a close and continuing coordination between users and the developers.

Finally, it should be noted that the problem of acquisition of basic urban data has not been stressed here. We recognize that the United States, with its large and careful census data, is probably quite wealthy in this regard. However, one of the main lessons we have relearned in developing the San Francisco model is the high degree of aggregation which is practical in studying many urban problems, provided a careful and appropriate model structure is available. Even in countries where the data base is far less developed than in the United States, we believe these models can receive useful application if they are properly designed, and can be supported by a limited amount of sampling of relevant population and housing characteristics.

References.

1. The Journal of the American Institute of Planners for May
    1965 contains summaries of many of these models.

2. "Model of San Francisco Housing Market," Technical Paper
    No. 8, submitted by Arthur D. Little, Inc. to the City of
    San Francisco, Community Renewal Program.

3. Notes on Operations Research 1959, Operations Research
    Center, M.I.T., The Technology Press, Massachusetts
    Institute of Technology, Cambridge, Mass., p. 1, 1959.

4. Black. D. M. and L. Winnick, "The Structure of the Housing
    Market," Quarterly Journal of Economics, 65, No. 2
    (1953)

Chapter 4

VEHICULAR TRAFFIC

Leslie C. Edie

4.1 Operations Research in The Port of New York Authority

This Chapter will illustrate the operations research methods
used at The Port of New York Authority for several of the operations conducted at its facilities. We shall begin, however, with
a brief outline of the scope of the Port Authority's responsibilities.

In 1921, the States of New York and New Jersey entered into
a treaty creating The Port of New York Authority. Under the
Port Compact, the Port Authority was charged with two basic
responsibilities -- the development and operation of transportation and terminal facilities in the Port District, an area within
a 25-mile radius of the Statue of Liberty, and the promotion and
protection of the commerce of the Port.

In carrying out its responsibilities, the Port Authority has
developed and operates twenty-three facilities, which include
six interstate tunnels and bridges, a regional system of four
airports and two heliports, six marine terminals, a bus terminal, two union motor truck terminals, and a truck terminal
for railroad freight. In addition, on September 1, 1962 the
Port Authority Trans-Hudson Corporation (PATH), a subsidiary
of The Port of New York Authority, acquired title to and began
operation of the Hudson Tubes, a vital rapid transit system
which links Newark, Jersey City and Hoboken with lower- and
mid-Manhattan. These facilities represent an investment of
over $1.5 billion. The entire program is carried out on a
self-supporting basis, without cost to the general taxpayer.

At present a major facility being constructed by the Port
Authority is The World Trade Center in lower Manhattan. It
comprises a project of major proportions designed to provide
a unified community in the New York-New Jersey Port District
for America's export-import business, and to act as a clearing
house for the handling, development, and expansion of such
business. The World Trade Center will feature twin towers of
gleaming metal, the tallest buildings in the world, soaring
110 stories, 1,350 feet, above a great open Plaza of almost
five acres, surrounded by four buildings, each with a specific

function in international trade.

The design of the tower buildings themselves and of their elevator systems are both novel, and the elevator system has been the subject of a recent operations research study at the Port Authority. The elevator system is known as the "Skylobby" system, which requires a fewer number of elevator shafts and makes available more usable areas in the buildings than in the conventionally equipped skyscrapers. It employs large, high-speed elevators to move passengers between the concourse level of the Center (immediately below the Plaza) and skylobbies at floors located about one third and two thirds of the height of the buildings. The buildings are thus divided into three elevator zones, each of which is then served by local elevators. The design and operation of this elevator system has been simulated on a computer by one of the Port Authority's research groups. [1] The results indicated that good elevator service can be provided with considerable savings in the percentage of floor space devoted to the elevator system.

The use of operations research techniques in the Port Authority dates back to 1952.[4] At present the Port Authority has three O.R. groups, the first of which was established in the Port Authority's industrial engineering group known as the Operations Standards Division. This division is a part of the Port Authority's internal consulting organization known as the Operations Services Department. The second O.R. group was founded in 1955 in the Tunnels and Bridges Department and is now a part of that department's research division. This division, which reports directly to the executive in charge of the department, handles projects involving the use of operations research and other scientific and technical methods to improve the operation and design of the tunnels and bridges facilities. The third O.R. group was established in 1961 in the Engineering Department. This group is concerned with applying operations research methods to long-range problems of major importance to the Port Authority as a whole or to a group of facilities. To supplement the work of these internal O.R. groups, the Authority has, from time to time, made use of outside part-time analysts and consultants.

4.2 Rational Toll-Lane Usage

The first example of a major operations research study that we shall consider deals with the management of the toll collection operations performed at the Authority's tunnels and bridges.[5] The collection of tolls at these facilities involves more than 250 toll collectors and annual operating costs of more than $2 \frac{1}{2}$ million dollars. The objective of this O.R. investigation was to improve the methods of managing the operation in an effort

to provide a high-level service to the public with the minimum
of cost. The problems involved in seeking this objective were
a queuing problem, to determine the relationship between the
number of toll collectors provided and the delay to patrons; an
optimizing problem, to determine the optimum level of service
and cost; and a scheduling problem, to find the most efficient
way in which to schedule reporting times and relief breaks for
the toll collectors, so that optimum service would be provided
with the minimum number of toll collectors. The results of
these studies were verified by field trials before the new method
was proposed to management.

In the queuing problem, we are interested in the lengths of
the queues in toll lanes in relation to the percentage of the time
the toll lanes are occupied by one or more vehicles. The general shape of the functional relationship was observed to be
that shown in Figure 4.1, where the variable u represents the

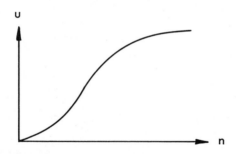

Figure 4. 1. System occupancy u vs. customers in the system n.

per cent of the time the toll lanes are occupied, and the variable
n represents the average number of vehicles in the system waiting to be served. For any particular level of occupancy, there
is a distribution around the average of the number of vehicles
waiting to be served. The probability density and distribution
functions were expected to have the features shown in Figures
4.2 and 4.3, respectively.

These relationships are typical of those found generally in
queuing problems. The question raised was: Did the toll-lane
operation fit any of the existing queuing models? To answer
this question, data were taken from all of the toll plazas on the
number of vehicles arriving at the toll lanes in 30-second intervals, and the queue lengths observed at the end of each such
interval. With one toll lane in service, the occupancy as a
function of the delay ratio showed a very good fit with the
Pollaczek-Crommelin theory for a single server with a constant
service-time distribution, as illustrated in Figure 4. 4.

p (n)

P (n ≥ x)

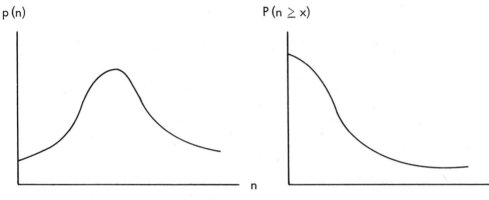

n

Figure 4.2. Probability
density p(n) vs. number
in the system n.

Figure 4.3. Probability
distribution.

OCCUPANCY %

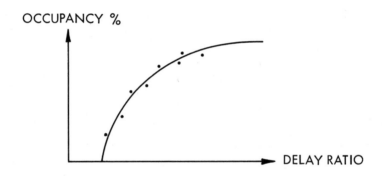

DELAY RATIO

Figure 4.4 Occupancy vs. delay in units of average
holding time.

    With more than one toll lane in service, however, classical
queuing theory was found to provide a poor estimation of the
delays observed. The reason for this is evidently the lack of
full availability of any toll lane to any vehicle. Full availability,
an assumption of the theories tested, is not obtained with toll
lanes because of the difficulties of maneuvering a vehicle into
an open toll lane far to the left or right. One of the interesting
findings relative to the operation of several toll lanes in parallel
was the inefficiency of right-hand toll lanes (collecting from the
side of the vehicle opposite the driver). In the reconstruction
of toll plazas, all of the right-hand lanes have been eliminated.
Another interesting finding, contrary to classical queuing theory,
was that the efficiency of servers in parallel did not increase
with larger and larger group sizes, but instead a maximum
efficiency was reached with four to six lanes in parallel.[6] This

result can be attributed to the increasing difficulty of drivers
finding and maneuvering into the lane with the shortest queue
as the number of lanes is increased. The increased efficiency
of the larger groups is more than offset by the maneuvering
problem.

In addition to the studies of the relationship between occupancy and average delay, it was considered desirable to estimate the probabilities of isolated inordinate delays. The usual
approach in queue problems is to determine the probability
density and distribution functions previously presented. Where
mathematical theory exists, the density and distribution functions are readily derivable from the parameters of the functions
involved. Where these are not available, it is conceivable that
the curves could be obtained from empirical data. This, however, would require the creation of excessive delay conditions
that would have been an imposition on the patrons. Fortunately,
the maximum queue length in any of the open toll lanes was
found to follow a Poisson distribution, viz.,

$$p(n \geq x) = \frac{e^{-m} m^x}{x!}$$

This meant that it was only necessary to determine empirically the value of the single parameter m in order to estimate
the probability of any queue length for a given number of toll
lanes and volume of traffic.

The most difficult problem to solve has been that of scheduling toll collectors to meet a demand for toll lanes that varied
frequently throughout the day, reaching morning and afternoon
peaks and falling to much lower levels of demand during the
middle part of the day and the evening. Such scheduling may
be done manually by preparing a histogram showing the number
of toll lanes required to meet service standards for each half
hour of the day (Figure 4.5).

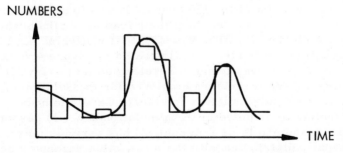

Figure 4.5. Number of toll lanes required compared to number
used in a day.

A Gantt type chart may be constructed by trial and error to
show the reporting time, quitting time, and work-break periods
for each toll collector. By adjusting the reporting times and
the breaks, one can seek to fulfill the requirements given by
histogram with the minimum number of toll collectors. Since
this is a very tedious and time-consuming process, continual
study has been given to the development of an algorithm which
would yield the toll-collector assignments with an optimal result. An algorithm is now available which is approximately
90 per cent efficient as compared with the best manual sched-
ulers. It is expected that the development of schedules for the
toll collectors will be fully automated in the near future. A
computer program will forecast the pattern of traffic demand
throughout the day, compute the number of toll lanes required
by half hours to meet the optimum standards of service, and
then prepare a schedule for the toll collectors to meet the service requirements with the minimum number of collectors.

Another problem that has been studied in the toll-collection
area has been that of the use of women to collect tolls in place
of police officers. The public acceptance of women collectors
has been very good, and the release of more than 250 police
officers to meet the growing requirements of traffic direction
and control, security of premises, protection of the public,
and so forth, at expanding and new Port Authority facilities,
has been valuable. A number of operations research studies
have been made in connection with these policing functions;[4]
one in particular resulted in the patrolling of Port Authority
tunnels at night by means of vehicles instead of the foot patrol
previously used. This method has demonstrated its effectiveness and has yielded annual savings of some $100,000.

4.3 Bus Terminal

This problem arose at the Port Authority's midtown bus terminal in Manhattan.[3] At the time, it was servicing 26,000 out-
bound commuters in one peak hour, 5-6 p.m., and had peak-
hour departures of about 450 buses. It was found that buses
were having difficulty reaching their loading berths because
they were blocked by other buses. Most platforms have five
holding spaces or berths, as illustrated in Figure 4.6, and the
blocking of buses was found to result when they arrive in incorrect order. The techniques employed for the solution of this
problem involved simulation and Monte Carlo methods.

The points to be noted in the simulation are: 1) passenger
arrivals (assumed to be Poisson), 2) bus arrivals (assumed to
be normally distributed with the mean value 9 minutes before
the scheduled departure time and a standard deviation of 5 minutes, 3) a bus-loading rate of 14 passengers per minute, 4) a

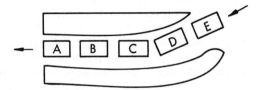

Figure 4.6. Multiple-berth bus-loading platform.

dispatching logic. The output of this simulation showed the
relationship between the number of loading berths per platform,
the number of holding spots per berth, and the average and
maximum delays to the passengers. Some results are given
below:

Berths	1 Holding Space		$\frac{1}{2}$ Holding Space	
	Average	Maximum	Average	Maximum
2	3.3	8.5	4.5	13.0
3	3.4	10.2	5.5	18.0
.	.	.	.	.
.	.	.	.	.
.	.	.	.	.
6	3.5	13.0	7.5	25.0

Before this study was undertaken, there were 13 holding spaces and 72 berths, which resulted in serious delays because of
the blocking effects. Consequently, holding places were added
at street level. This significantly reduced the congestion on
the suburban level and the delays to passengers. When this bus
terminal was expanded, single-berth platforms of the pull-in
back-out type were constructed to avoid the blockage problem.
The results of the study also were utilized in the design of the
George Washington Bridge Bus Station, which was provided
with platforms having three berths, and with a number of holding spaces equal to the number of berths.

4.4 Telephone Information Service

The Bus Terminal telephone information service was studied
in the interest of improving the service, reducing the costs, or
both.[7] It was found that the information calls originate at random

and are not influenced by bus schedules. The call length was
observed to have a negative exponential distribution and, therefore, fit exactly a queuing theory derived by Dr. Riordan of the
Bell Telephone Laboratories. Optimum levels of service were
found to involve an average answering delay of 15 seconds and
maximum delay (p = 0.05) of 75 seconds. It was found that the
scheduling of telephone-information-agent tours based on these
standards of service could provide a more uniform grade of
service in addition to operating savings of approximately
$25,000 per year. The cost of the study amounted to approxi-
mately $8,000.

4.5 Rapid Transit System

The rapid transit system that the Port Authority has acquired
at the request of the State of New Jersey was formerly known
as the Hudson and Manhattan Railroad. It is now called PATH,
the acronym for the Port Authority Trans-Hudson Corporation.
The Port Authority acquired the rapid transit system after many
years of bankruptcy; the system was plagued with obsolescence,
poorly maintained equipment, and frequent breakdowns. There
were too few cars to permit adequate maintenance, nearly all
of them being required on line to handle peak-hour traffic.

A simulation model was used for studying the scheduling of
the trains in the system.[2] The model had subroutines for gen-
erating passenger arrivals at each station, the loading time at
the station, and the travel time between stations. To determine
the most important objectives in the scheduling of trains, passengers using the system were questioned and were found to be
interested in reliability, comfort, making desired connections,
and speed, in that order. The trips being short, about five to
six miles, speed was found to be of least importance. These
passenger criteria were used to select the best of a number of
alternate schedules. It was found that the number of cars required to carry the peak-hour traffic could be reduced and still
provide a better service from the passenger's point of view.
The release of these cars then permitted improved maintenance
and a reduction in the frequency of breakdown of the old cars,
until such time as new cars could be procured. The simulation
model gave the train size, passenger inventory, timing, proportion of waiting passengers boarding, and the interference
between trains at junction points.

The same simulation model has been used to update the train
schedules from time to time as new cars have been put into
service and as passenger demands have changed. Simulation
has proved to be an effective method for dealing with problems
of this kind, and has the advantage that it is more readily understood by managers of the operations than are analytical solutions.

4.6 Tunnel Congestion

A cursory examination of traffic flow in a tunnel lane would suggest that vehicles could safely travel at 35 miles an hour with a spacing of 75 feet between vehicles. Under such conditions a flow of 2,100 vehicles per lane per hour could be sustained. The actual rate of flow observed, however, is in the range of 1,000 to 1,200 vehicles per lane, i.e., with an average around 1,100. To determine why the actual flow rate is only about one half of that which could be reasonably expected required the development of traffic-flow theory and experimental methods to study driver-vehicle interaction and the traffic dynamics in relation to the geometry of the tunnel. A useful analogy can be drawn between the behavior of vehicular traffic in a tunnel and fluid in a channel.

If a pipe holds 2 gallons of water per foot length and the water flows at 100 feet/minute, the resulting flow is 200 feet/minute, i.e., $q = kv$ (Figure 4.7). The same will hold for a uniform

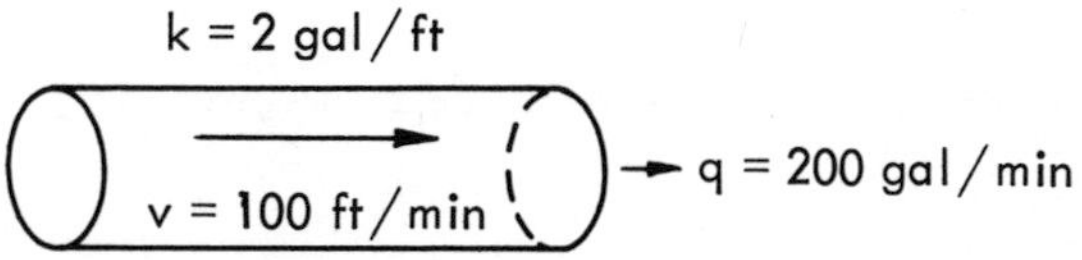

$$k = 2 \text{ gal}/\text{ft}$$

$$v = 100 \text{ ft}/\text{min} \qquad q = 200 \text{ gal}/\text{min}$$

Figure 4.7. Fluid analogy to traffic flow.

flow of vehicles, with k standing for cars/mile, and v for miles/hour or some suitable units. For a nonuniform flow, a space-weighted average of speeds gives

$$\bar{v} = \frac{q}{k} = \frac{\Sigma k_i u_i}{\Sigma k_i}$$

An alternative observational definition was suggested in 1955 by the British physicists, Lighthill and Whitham. Observing the number of cars n passing across a short increment dx of the roadway over a long period of time T, and the times dt_i taken by the cars to cross the distance dx, we should define

$$q = \frac{n}{T}, \qquad u = \frac{\Sigma n dx}{\Sigma dt_i}, \qquad k = \frac{q}{u}$$

If the observation post is moving upstream at speed c, we shall have

$$q + ck = \frac{n}{T}$$

and if moving downstream

$$q - ck = \frac{n}{T}$$

Thus an experiment of traveling at two different speeds will enable one to estimate the flow rate. If two cars travel together with a constant time separation,

$$q_i - ck_i = \frac{n}{T} \qquad i = 1, 2$$

will give a "wave" traveling on the roadway at speed

$$c = \frac{q_2 - q_1}{k_2 - k_1}$$

The "wave front" can be depicted as in Figure 4.8.

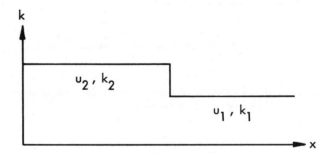

Figure 4.8. Change of state in a traffic stream from speed and concentration u_2, k_2 to u_1, k_1 downstream from a wave front.

The "Principle of Conservation of Cars" will give an inflow = outflow equation for the wave

$$(u_2 - c) k_2 = (u_1 - c) k_1$$

Thus, on a q-k diagram, the speed $c = \frac{dq}{dk}$ of the wave speed $\frac{q}{k}$ of the vehicles can be seen at once (Figure 4.9).

Using the kind of theoretical approach described above, in conjunction with experiments giving quantitative values for the

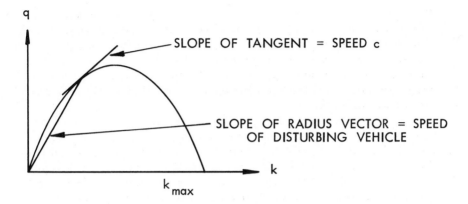

Figure 4. 9. Flow (q) vs. concentration (k) in a traffic
stream showing the wave speed (c), the
slope of the tangent, and the traffic speed,
the slope of the radius vector.

wave velocities and the shape of the flow concentration curve,
it has been feasible to design traffic control systems for tunnel
lanes which will improve the peak-hour flow rate and reduce
the travel time through the tunnel.[8,9,10] In addition, these control methods have been found to reduce the incidence of vehicular breakdowns and to reduce the ventilation requirements for
the tunnels. Several traffic control methods have been used in
the field, and the equipment has been continually improved for
more effective performance.

The amount of increase in flow obtained, however, has so
far been a nominal 5 per cent. It is anticipated that this can
be increased, but even a 5 per cent improved peak-hour capacity can reduce the aggregate delays to motorists using tunnels
by as much as 60 to 70 per cent. Efforts are now being made
by other organizations to extend the use of this type of traffic
control to freeways as well as tunnels.

4.7 Summary

Several types of operations research studies made at the
Port Authority have been discussed briefly. Some of these,
like the management of the toll collection operation and the
improvement of traffic flow, are studies of a continuing nature.
Other studies, like the Bus Terminal simulation and the policing of tunnels by motor vehicles instead of by foot, have provided the answers needed by management without the necessity
for further research.

Some of the newer areas of operations research that are now

under way include urban land-use and transportation models, an analysis of contracting procedures, and investigations into methods of defining and measuring service in the transportation context. These are of a long-range, basic nature, and extend the use of O.R. into complex operations. A number of short-range specific problems continue to be handled as they arise from time to time.

Operations research has demonstrated its usefulness in contributing to the solution of problems in transportation. This result is leading to the development of a new field of scientific endeavor which has become known as "Transportation Science." It is to be expected that this field will grow and that an increasing number of our transportation problems will be made tractable to solution by quantitative methods.

References

1. Browne, J., and J. Kelly, "Simulation of the World Trade Center Elevator System," IEEE, New York Chapter Meeting, March 15, 1967.

2. Browne, J., "Simulation Scores for PATH," Modern Railroads, October, 1966.

3. Dickins, J. H., and N. H. Jennings, "Computer Simulation of Peak Hour Operations in a Bus Terminal," Management Science, 5, No. 1, 106-120 (October, 1958).

4. Edie, L. C., "Operations Research in a Public Corporation," Operations Research, 5, No. 1, 111-122 (February, 1957).

5. Edie, L. C., "Traffic Delays at Toll Booths," Operations Research, 2, No. 2, 107-138 (May, 1954).

6. Edie, L. C., "Review of Port of New York Authority Study," Operations Research, 8, No. 2, 263-277 (March, 1960).

7. Edie, L. C., "Planning and Control of Service Operations," Proceedings, Operations Research in Industry Symposium, University of Michigan, Ann Arbor, Michigan, June, 1957.

8. Edie, L. C., "Real Time Traffic Control," Proceedings, Computer Applications Symposium, Chicago, 1962, Spartan Books, Baltimore, 1964.

9. Foote, R. S., "Single Lane Traffic Flow Control," Proceedings, Second International Symposium on Theory of Traffic Flow, O.E.C.D., Paris, 1965.

10. Greenberg, H., and A. Daou, "The Control of Traffic Flow to Increase the Flow," Operations Research, 8, No. 4, 524-532 (July, 1960).

Chapter 5

THE EVALUATION OF
ALTERNATIVE TRANSPORTATION NETWORKS*

Peter S. Loubal

5.1 Introduction

Transportation planning begins with a massive data-collection effort, in order to ascertain the existing travel patterns in their dependence on the characteristics of the travellers, the transportation system, and the nature of land-use activities at the origins and destinations of trips. Additional data and trend information are required for forecasting future population and employment, industrial development, urban growth patterns, etc.

The collection, reduction, and analysis of this massive amount of data have been made possible only by the advent of the computer.

The major sources of financing are, at the Federal level, based mainly on the 1961 Housing Act, which provides for funds to be devoted to comprehensive planning in urban regions; the 1962 Federal Highway Act, which requires that at least 1½ per cent of federal-aid funds be spent on planning and research; and the Urban Mass Transit Act of 1964, which provides assistance for capital improvements to transit systems. At the local level the financing comes mainly from local portions of gas-tax revenues and from special bond issues.

The 1962 Highway Act provided that every urban area of 50,000 or more population must have a continuing, comprehensive, and coordinated planning process by July 1, 1965, to qualify for Federal highway aid. Currently, this requirement is being met by over 200 metropolitan areas throughout the country.

In the San Francisco Bay Area a Transportation Study Commission was created in 1963 and charged specifically with the conduct of a comprehensive transportation study, the preparation of a master regional transportation plan, and with recommending ways and means of implementing the plan. The cost

---

* This Chapter is based on a report by Peter S. Loubal entitled, "A Network Evaluation Procedure," August, 1966, submitted to the Bay Area Transportation Commission.

of such a study over a three-year period was estimated at approximately \$4,500,000 -- about \$1.00 per capita, based on the 1965 population estimate for the region.

The study is supervised by a Commission representing the public-at-large and various counties and cities in the area; it is assisted by a Citizens' Advisory Committee and the study staff. Technical coordination with other agencies and groups of the area is fostered through advisory committees and engineering councils.

The methodology of any transportation study is based on the basic premise that there is a basic regularity and orderliness in the lives of large numbers of people; overall travel patterns can thus be established and simulated by mathematical models on computers, so that both present and expected future behavior can be reproduced. Appropriate systems of transportation can then be planned to meet the anticipated demand. Planning for large systems requires the investigation of a wide variety of possible combinations, and this cannot easily be done if each must be arduously described in great detail. However, many planning questions can be analyzed in some measure at a gross level in order to define effective system combinations and to exclude the proposals not worthy of searching examination.

A major purpose of any transportation study is the evaluation of all important transportation projects, such as bridges, transit lines, tunnels, and freeways, on the basis of their benefits and costs, taking into account other social, political, and general economic factors.

Since various projects can compete for traffic or cooperate in carrying traffic (often doing both at the same time, depending upon the origins and destinations of the various trips), the total benefit of several projects cannot be assessed as the simple sum of the benefits of these projects taken individually. This is in direct contrast to the total cost of these projects, which will, in general, be the sum cost of the individual projects.

Since available investment funds are always limited, not all projects can be built, and it therefore becomes imperative to evaluate the costs and benefits of as many realistic project combinations and alternatives as possible. The sum of all possible project combinations is, however, an extremely high number equal to

$$\sum_k \binom{n}{k} = 2^n,$$

where n is the number of projects. There are therefore in theory more than 1,000 possible project combinations for 10 projects, more than 1,000,000 for 20 projects, and more than 1,000,000,000 for 30 projects.

This Chapter will suggest guidelines for reducing the problem as well as discuss some of the methods of solution.

5.2 Traffic Estimation

We will first discuss briefly some of the prerequisites for network evaluation. In view of the purpose of our efforts, it is reasonable to begin with some estimation of the present and future demands for and usage of the facilities we contemplate. From these we would hope to extract parameter values of interest in composing a criterion of optimality in the selection of present and future projects.

First there is the process of Traffic Generation, which establishes the amount of traffic produced by or attracted to all major areas in the region under study. This largely involves estimation of population at various locations, migration habits, employment requirements, and land use. Statistical and socioeconomic studies can also be carried out to account for more actual factors affecting stability and growth of population.

The next phase of the estimation process is the Traffic Distribution phase, input to which would be those facts learned from the Traffic Generation phase. For instance, using our population estimates in different areas, we try to predict various traffic desires or demands between them. Let us examine briefly some models used in connection with this.

First there is the Fratar model,[7] which assumes that the populations and transportation network remain fairly constant. As an example of the approach let us suppose that the existing travel desires in both directions between three zones in a region are known; they are represented by the values on the links of Figure 5.1a. The total number of trip-ends for each zone are given in the nodes of Figure 5.1a. If it is now assumed that future changes in population, employment, etc., will lead to given increases in the number of trip-ends in each zone, with say 70 trip-ends in zone a, 60 trip-ends in zone b, and 110 trip-ends in zone c, for some future date (Figure 5.1b), the Fratar procedure will provide the resulting interzonal travel flows, represented by the values on the links of Figure 5.1b, based on the assumption that existing travel desires can be extrapolated.

The technique is not readily amenable to a situation where new zones have to be created, e.g., for major new residential developments or when major changes are made to the transportation network.

Next there is the Gravity model, which relates the traffic between two points to the distance between them by a gravitational law resembling that of Newton:

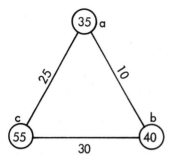

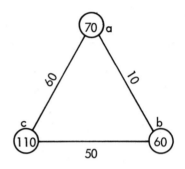

Figure 5. 1a. Existing interzonal   Figure 5. 1b. Predicted interzonal
              travel desires.   travel desires.

$$t_{ij} = \frac{\rho_{ij} P_i A_j}{d_{ij}^x} \tag{5.1}$$

where t_{ij} = total number of trips from i to j

ρ_{ij} = some constant of proportionality

P_i = trips produced by i $\Big\}$ (derived from

A_j = trips attracted to j $\Big\}$ Generation phase)

d_{ij} = distance (or time) between i and j

A more general model is the following:

$$t_{ij} = \frac{P_i A_j d_{ij}^x}{\sum_j A_j d_{ij}^x} \tag{5.2}$$

This model is applicable to more general situations than
Fratar's and allows addition of new links to the network.

5.3 Traffic Assignment

   From the Distribution phase we are thus able to obtain, by
iterative procedures if necessary, a trip table of elements t_{ij}
indicating the magnitude of traffic demand in the i-j direction.
Where there are a large number of towns or localities it is
then possible, by examination of the trip table, to single out
major traffic links and regard all other facilities as existing
within zonal areas, which we then represent by suitable nodes.
Thus we prepare to take a macroscopic view of the original
network, reducing it to a set of zones within which traffic is

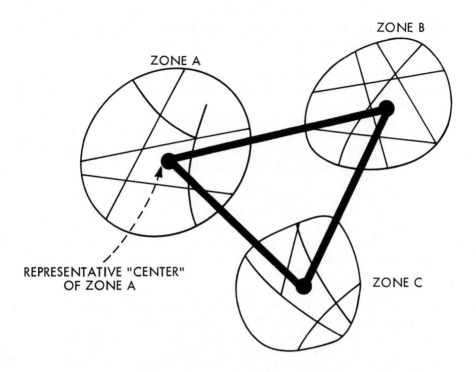

Figure 5.2. Intrazonal and interzonal connections.

assumed to be light compared to that on interzonal links.   This
is illustrated in Figure 5.2.

It is then feasible that a trip table for this new macronetwork
is derivable from the original trip table.   This will be used in
the Network Evaluation process.   In addition, a travel time
table is constructed that gives travel times between zones under
the assumption of free flow of traffic without congestion.   In the
event of congestion, however, we have also to take into account
the capacity c_{ij} of the link from i to j.   The underlying prin-
ciples on which assignment of traffic is based are these:

1. Traffic adapts very quickly to the quickest route available;
2. Traffic will continue to take the quickest path until conges-
    tion makes some other path quickest.   (Wardrop's Second
    Principle.)

The first principle leads us to evaluate for each pair of zones
the quickest path connecting them under free flow.   Let us denote by $S(i,j)$ such a path for the nodes i, j.   Methods for finding these paths are well known, and in particular there is an
algorithm due to Moore which begins with a set consisting only

of the node i, say, and by a fanning-out process includes the next node that is nearest to the existing set, and records its shortest distance from i. The procedure is continued until all nodes are included.

If there still remains a pair of nodes for which the shortest distance is not yet found, the procedure would then be repeated for that pair.

The procedure is very fast and programs for running on IBM 7094 and CDC 3600 computers are available, capable of determining the shortest path between one point of a network and several thousand others in approximately one second of computer time.

Thus if we ignore congestion and capacity constraints and assume what is known as "all or nothing" loading (where a path considered to be optimal between two zones is used by all traffic between those zones), then the above model suffices for assignment of traffic. It is to be observed, however, that link cost need not be just travel time, as we have used so far, but may include consideration of congestion, tolls, accident incidence, and other travel-resisting factors; the above model still provides us with a least-cost assignment.

In consideration of the second principle, we may choose to divide the total traffic flow into two or more routes between origin and destination, depending on the relative values of travel resistances and capacities on the routes. As an illustration, we may consider two adjacent zones having two alternative interconnecting routes, e. g. , a freeway and an arterial highway, where the distance via the freeway is usually much greater than via the arterial. Figure 5.3 demonstrates the effect of congestion; it shows the graphical relation between the percentage of traffic that uses the freeway and the ratio of "congested" travel times on freeway versus arterial.

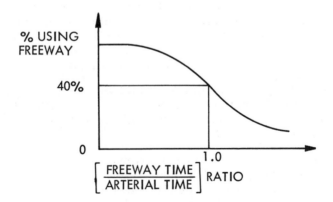

Figure 5.3. The effect of congestion.

Figure 5.4 demonstrates the effect of capacity in causing such congestion. Here we see that travel time increases rapidly as the traffic flow approaches the capacity on any given route.

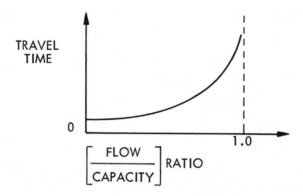

Figure 5.4. The effect of capacity in causing congestion.

In an effort then to make a reasonable assignment of traffic along two alternative routes, a and b, say, we may try to minimize the total time

$$t = f_a t_a + (1 - f_a) t_b \tag{5.3}$$

by suitable choice of f_a, (and $f_b = 1 - f_a$) where $t_a = t_a(f_a)$ and $t_b = t_b(f_b)$ are relations of the type shown in Figure 5.4. The problem may be represented graphically as shown in Figure 5.5.

For such a problem it is well known that there is a solution giving minimal "combined" time.

5.4 Evaluating Alternative Networks

We next examine the problem of evaluating projects or proposed modification of existing networks. In general such propositions may involve building new links or improving old ones, thereby changing their congestion characteristics. As a simple case let us look at a project involving a single new link. We then have to determine the zone pairs between which the new "shortest" path includes the new project. This would assist us in making new traffic assignments and obtain new patterns of congestions for further study. For this problem a special tree-building process is available which is a slight modification of the Moore algorithm already mentioned. The only differences are as follows:

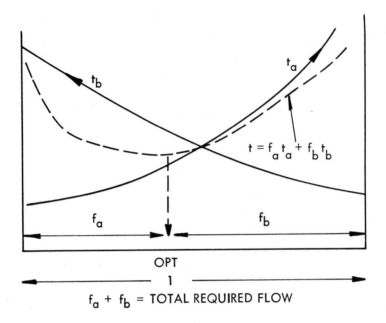

Figure 5.5. Minimization of the function $t_a(f_a, f_b) \equiv$
$f_a \cdot t_a(f_a) + f_b \cdot t_b(f_b)$ (dotted line) over
the region $f_a + f_b = 1$.

1. Two or more "project" nodes -- either the end nodes of a
   "project" link or several nodes representing the interchanges of a segment of freeway or the stops of a transit
   line segment -- are used as "home" nodes or origins at
   the start of the process, so that two or more disjoint tree
   branches are obtained.
2. Whenever a node is reached in the tree-building process,
   it is labeled by a subset or tree branch number to indicate
   from which home node the branch originated.

The procedure is just as efficient as the fastest standard tree-
building process and has the same computer core requirements.
    At the end of the tree-building process a project-tree is ob-
tained (see Figure 5.6) consisting of two or more branches, so
that each node is connected with the closest project node. In
case of equal travel times, one or the other project node is
selected. (It is, of course, also possible to minimize distances,
costs, or some other value.)
    The project tree has the following properties:

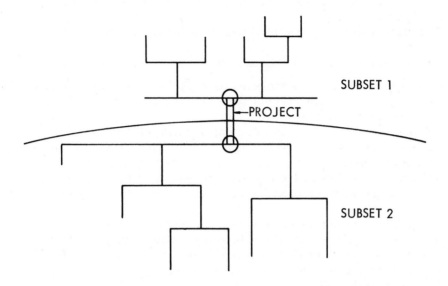

Figure 5.6. Simplified sketch illustrating project tree
          having two branches.

1. No two nodes belonging to the same branch, that is, having
   the same subset number, can be connected by a minimal
   path that would include the project link, since their connection via the last common node on their branch cannot be
   longer than the sum of the shortest distances between them
   and the closer project node.
2. Only the paths between the nodes of different branches
   could possibly have been improved by the inclusion of the
   project link. Therefore only these connections will have
   to be tested.
3. The minimal path between nodes, each belonging to separate subsets, via the project link(s), can easily be determined by summing the times from the two project nodes
   and the time required to cross the project link(s). The
   project link time therefore does not enter the actual tree-
   building process and can be varied depending upon various
   conditions; for instance, it could be adjusted to reflect
   traffic flows, different tolls, etc.

For a single project, the output of the tree-building process
can be used to:

1. Limit the number of pairwise zone connections which need
   to be tested for possible time savings achieved due to the
   inclusion of a project.

2. Determine the via-project time savings or losses for these pairs of zones.
3. Determine the flow diverted to the project, given a trip table.
4. Determine the flow changes for base network links.

These tasks can be performed by very fast and simple steps involving base network travel time and trip tables, and the project tree output table.

Subset labels s_i are used for determining the two sets of zones (nodes) which should be evaluated. The via-project times between all pairs of zones of these subsets (one from each subset) are easily determined by summing the two times from the closer project node and adding the time needed to cross the project link.

Actually it is not necessary to evaluate travel times between all zones of the two subsets, since if no time saving is achieved by travel across a project to a particular zone from the zones of the other subset, then no zone on the branch behind it can achieve a time saving.

5.5 Sample Problem

The node values at the beginning and end of the procedure on a small sample network are shown in Figure 5.7. As can be seen, the minimum path between nodes 2 and 13 via the project link (7, 11) is 16(5+3+8) (which in this case is larger than the minimal path between them), while the path between the nodes 2 and 15 via the project will be 15(5$\overset{+}{-}$3$\overset{+}{-}$7) (which is also the minimal path between the two nodes). It can be clearly seen that there is no possibility that the path between any two nodes belonging to the same branch (e.g., nodes 2 and 12) could have been improved by including the project link, since the path following the in-tree links (2-3-7-8-9-12) must be better than any path via the project link.

The node subset number s_i can also be used to indicate the paths routed via some other link or links (possibly another project), so as to facilitate the evaluation of the interdependency between two or more projects. For instance, if an additional node were placed between nodes 3 and 4 and initialized at $s_i = 10$ (in binary notation), then at the end of the tree-building process, in the example illustrated in Figure 5.7b, the node subset numbers would be $s_3 = 00$, $s_4 = 10$, $s_1 = 10$, with the other s_i unchanged. This would indicate that only nodes 1 and 4 <u>could</u> lie on a minimum path connecting nodes 1 and/or 4 with nodes 10, 11, 13, 14, and 15.

It is also possible to initialize the project end nodes (3, 4), without using an intermediate node, to achieve the same

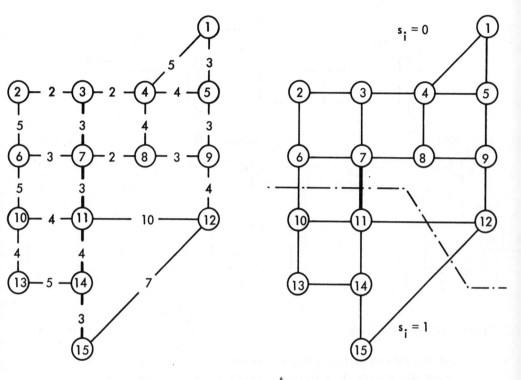

Figure 5.7. Sample network, with $\frac{t_i}{s_i}$ values before (a) and after (b), building a project tree for link (7, 11).

(a) Circled numbers are node designations, numbers on links are travel times; $t_i = 999$, $s_i = 0$, except for "project" nodes 7 and 11 with $t_7 = 0$, $s_7 = 0$, $t_{11} = 0$, $s_{11} = 1$.

(b) The subset numbers s_i are indicated on the network. The distances from the closer "project" node are: $t_1 = 10$, $t_2 = 5$, $t_3 = 3$, $t_4 = 5$, $t_5 = 8$, $t_6 = 3$, $t_7 = 0$, $t_8 = 2$, $t_9 = 5$, $t_{10} = 4$, $t_{11} = 0$, $t_{12} = 9$, $t_{13} = 8$, $t_{14} = 4$, $t_{15} = 7$.

purpose. In this case two binary bits per link would be required to indicate whether a path leads through the project link or not. In the example of Figure 5.7b, initializing $s_3 = 010$, $s_4 = 010$, the new subset numbers at the end of the process would be $s_4 = 100$, $s_i = 100$, indicating that the tree was built through the link (3, 4).

To save tree-building time for projects composed of a series of links, such as freeways or transit lines, these can be treated by building project trees from several project nodes simultaneously with each project node initialized at a unique s_i value (see Figure 5.8). The travel time via a project is then the sum

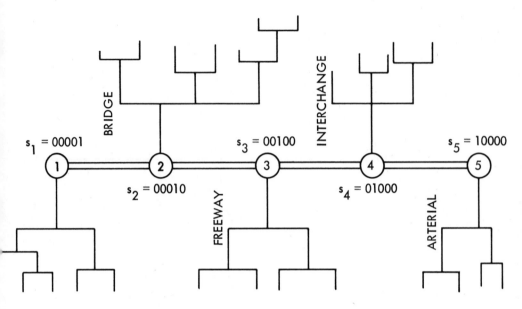

Figure 5. 8. Illustrating tree-building when projects are serially linked.

of the minimum-path travel times to the closest project nodes plus the travel time between these project nodes. Again, the nodes belonging to the same branch need not be evaluated. In the case where this method would lead to errors due to the existence of a shorter path via a project node in the direction of travel (rather than the closest project node), it is recommended that two project trees be built. For the example indicated in Figure 5. 8, one tree would be built for nodes 1, 3, 5, and the other built for nodes 2 and 4. A proper evaluation of the two trees would tend to eliminate the possibility of the mentioned error.

5. 6 Multi-Project (Link) Evaluation

Projects can interact in a complex manner, since various projects can either compete for traffic, or cooperate in carrying traffic, or, as often occurs, do both at the same time, depending on the origins and destinations of the various trips. The total time savings due to the inclusion of several projects therefore cannot be assessed from the time-saving tables of the individual projects.

Take, for instance, two projects "a" and "b". Depending on their location and the other network values, some zone pair interchanges will not benefit from either of them, others from just one of the projects, and still others from both. With regard to this last possibility the projects could be (for a certain zone pair t_{ij}) in "series" and the time saving achieved by both projects will be greater than that achieved singly, i. e. :

$$d_{ij}^{ab} > (d_{ij}^a \, , \, d_{ij}^b) \tag{5.4}$$

or, the projects might be "parallel," and

$$d_{ij}^{ab} = \max (d_{ij}^a \, , \, d_{ij}^b) \tag{5.5}$$

in which case they might cooperate in carrying the flow between zones i and j, but compete with regard to time savings.

The following notation can conveniently be used in designating project trees:

$\overline{ab}$ = a project tree built for project b, with project a added to the base network.

$t_{ij}^{a\overline{b}}$ = the via-project a time, based on project tree $\overline{ab}$, with all zones on either side of project b evaluated.

$D_{\overline{ab}} = \{d_{ij}^{a\overline{b}}\}$ = the time-saving table, composed of $d_{ij}^{a\overline{b}} > 0$ elements $d_{ij}^{a\overline{b}} = t_{ij} - t_{ij}^{a\overline{b}}$

The time-saving table for project combination a, b can easily be determined as

$$
\begin{aligned}
D_{ab} &= \max (D_{\overline{a}}, \, D_{\overline{ab}}), \text{ or} \\
&= \max (D_{\overline{b}}, \, D_{\overline{ba}}), \text{ or} \\
&= \max (D_{a\overline{b}}, \, D_{b\overline{a}}) \tag{5.6}
\end{aligned}
$$

with the larger of the two elements of the component tables used to form the combination time-saving table.

It would also be possible to evaluate the time savings between zones on both sides of the two projects only. Denoting the resulting time-saving table as $D_{\underline{ab}}$, then also

$$D_{ab} = \max (D_{\overline{a}}, \, D_{\overline{b}}, \, D_{\underline{ab}}) \tag{5.7}$$

The difference between $D_{\underline{ab}}$ and $D_{\overline{ab}}$ is indicated in Figure 5.9.

With the two end nodes of project a initialized at s_k = 00,
s_1 = 01, and the project b node at s_m = 10, three subsets of
zones will be obtained in case the tree builds through project
link b. Time-saving table $D\overline{ab}$ is obtained by evaluating all
zones with s_i = 01 or 11 against those with s_i = 00, while
only the zones with s_i = 11 and s_i = 00 need to be checked
for $D\underline{a}\overline{b}$.

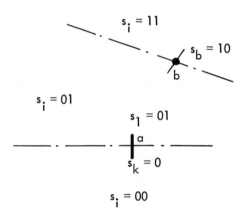

Figure 5.9. Sketch of difference between $D_{a\overline{b}}$ and $D_{\underline{a}\overline{b}}$.

Flows f_{ij} are assigned to a project link whenever its component time-saving table contributes a particular d_{ij} element
to the project combination time-saving table.

Therefore, in order to determine the effect of a combination
of several projects, only as many minimum-path trees as there
are single-link projects need be built, possibly with some additional trees required for multi-link projects. Furthermore,
the effect of the gradual inclusion of one project after another
can be evaluated in the process. So, for instance, if it is desired to determine the effect of including new or improved links
c, d, f, l, m in a network, only five minimum-path trees need be
built and, in the process, the effect of individual project combinations, such as d, df, dfm, dfmc, can also be ascertained.

In case it would later be necessary to evaluate the project
combination adfm, only a single additional tree would have to
be built, since projects dfm would have been evaluated earlier.

When it is desired to evaluate several hundred network alternatives, some of them composed of twenty or thirty project
links or of select existing links on which the flows are to be
monitored, it is necessary to sequence the project tree-building

and evaluation operations rationally. This is because the multi-
project alternatives will have common subsets of projects, possibly again project combinations which are to be tested. In
general, a rational network-evaluation sequence should not have
network alternatives differing by more than several projects
from some other alternative, since any major plan can only be
implemented gradually, and the effect of partial completion
should also be evaluated.

If it is nevertheless necessary to evaluate some alternative
network, differing to a large degree from any other alternative,
it is always possible to treat it as a new base network and to
apply the standard traffic-assignment procedure. The project
tree builder can then be used for evaluating slight changes to
the basically different new network.

5.7 Benefit/Cost Evaluation

We now examine a procedure for the gross evaluation of a
large number of alternative projects.

The cost (in dollars) of a network alternative is the sum of
the costs of all new projects in the given alternative, such as
construction costs, operating and maintenance costs, disloca-
tion costs, etc., adjusted to a common scale suitable for purposes of comparison. The adjustment should utilize discounting
and different interest rates, to take into account the fact that
projects will be built at different times in the future under different financing schemes. Additional factors that can be evaluated in dollars, such as revenue (bridge tolls, transit operation
profits) or accident costs, can easily be included. As can be
seen, some costs could be negative (i.e., revenue) but, in
general, a total project cost will be positive (outlay).

Benefits will be measured in time units, the major benefit
being the cumulative time saving in man-hours for satisfying
given travel demands due to a project or project combination.

The use of a time/cost space for a comparison of benefits
and cost of alternatives is a novel, though certainly not original,
idea. The arguments in favor of this selection of basic evaluation scales are very briefly the following:

In the first approach, evaluation of a large number of alternatives, the human mind can relatively easily operate with two
values, and in urban transportation those of cost and time are
probably the most meaningful ones. It is difficult to combine
the various cost elements, but the combination of cost and time
values on the basis of a time/cost factor is still more difficult.
In the contemplated evaluation process, the two basic measures
of time and cost are therefore left separate until the final analysis. For comparing a limited number of alternatives, the in-
gredients that went into the study of the "cost" (such as

construction, operating costs) and time saving (e.g., travel, terminal time) of several alternatives can, of course, be called for and viewed in detail.

The benefit/cost evaluation process can best be shown on a small example. Assume that all combination possibilities of four projects "a", "b", "c", and "d" have been evaluated; their respective benefits in time savings and costs, as shown in the accompanying Table 5.1, have been plotted in Figure 5.10.

Table 5.1. Benefits and Costs of All Combinations of
Four-Project Example

Seq. No.	Projects	Benefit	Cost
1	0	0	0
2	a	40	30
3	a, b	50	40
4	a, c	50	50
5	a, d	70	50
6	a, b, c	80	60
7	a, b, d	80	60
8	a, c, d	70	70
9	a, b, c, d	100	80
10	b	10	10
11	b, c	60	30
12	b, d	50	30
13	b, c, d	90	50
14	c	20	20
15	c, d	50	40
16	d	30	20

The cost of the individual projects is a: 30, b: 10, c: 20, d: 20 units.

The maximal benefit is obtained by building all four projects, which also entails the largest investment costs. The sequence in which the projects should be constructed so as to maximize benefits at any stage of completion is indicated by the line 1-10-11-13-9 for the project sequence b-c-d-a. If, for instance, only thirty units of investment were available, then project combination 11 (projects b, c) should be chosen. In the case that,

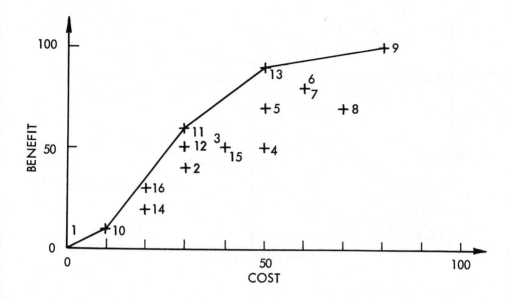

Figure 5.10. Benefits and costs of project combinations,
identified by sequence number (see Table 5.1).

due to esthetic, political, or other considerations, project combination 12 (b, d) is selected instead, the implication would be
that these "intangible" considerations have at least a value of
10 units of benefit.

It must be emphasized that the evaluation procedure suggested
here is to be used only for a rapid determination of the network
alternatives which should be investigated in greater detail, not
as a tool for reaching any final decision as to an "optimal" alternative. Nevertheless, the benefit/cost values for network alternatives can conveniently be utilized for a more detailed analysis
which, despite the fact that the data are gross, might be helpful
in eliminating the less promising alternatives. For instance,
the marginal effect of adding a particular project to, or removing
it from, some project combination can easily be determined from
the graph (Figure 5.10). Another value which can easily be found
is the maximum benefit/cost ratio r_{max}, which is the point of
tangency to a line leading through the origin (0 benefit, 0 investment cost). This is shown in Figure 5.11 for the same example.
The alternative with the highest benefit/cost ratio for any particular value of time r is the one farthest from the r line
(Figure 5.11).

It is difficult to evaluate all combinations of a larger number
of projects. The method suggested here is to determine a priori
the project combinations which should be evaluated, rank the

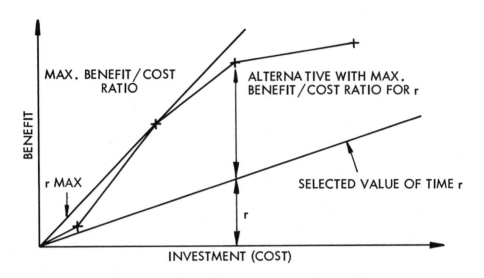

Figure 5.11. Values on the project evaluation curve.

results in the benefit/cost space, and then possibly decide on
other combinations which should also be evaluated. It is, of
course, always possible that in the use of this simple procedure,
some "optimal" combinations might be missed. This problem
has been considered by Kuhn[3] and by Ridley[5] with particular
regard to transportation, and by Weingartner[7] as a general
capital budgeting problem. In Appendix C there is described a
matrix method[4] which, on the basis of some simplifying assumptions, can evaluate all combinations of a larger number of projects. Since the procedure suggested in this report is used only
for the secondary task of evaluating network alternatives, but
not for the primary task of determining in some exact manner
alternatives that should be evaluated, these methods will not be
discussed in detail. Nevertheless, the present network-
evaluation procedure can conveniently be used for providing the
data necessary for the evaluation of any project combination, and it
would be of value to define properly a suitable primary objective:
To determine from all possible network alternatives and project
combinations those that maximize the benefit for any particular
level of investment. In the example of Figure 5.10, where all
combinations were listed, the optimal combinations would be:
b, d, bc, bcd, abcd for investment levels of 10, 20, 30, 50,
and 80 units, respectively.

The mathematical statement of the problem follows:

Minimize

$$t_k \cdot f = \sum_\ell t_k \cdot f_\ell \qquad\qquad (5.8)$$

constrained by

$$M \cdot f_\ell = q_\ell \qquad\qquad (5.9)$$

for a large number of diverse t_k; $k = 0, 1, 2\ldots\ldots, 2^n-1$.
In particular for such t_k, that if a value B_k is associated with
t_k and the label k is chosen in such a manner that $k' < k''$
implies $B_{k'} < B_{k''}$, then

$$t_{k'} \cdot f \geq t_{k''} \cdot f \qquad\qquad (5.10)$$

Notation:

  M = network incidence matrix

  t_k = time (cost) vector for iteration (project combinations)k

  f_ℓ = minimizing flow vector for centroid ℓ

  q_ℓ = node supply (demand) vector for centroid ℓ, i.e., a
    vector whose ℓ^{th} element (flow entering network at
    centroid ℓ) is non-negative, and the other elements
    (flows leaving the network at other centroids) are non-
    positive.

  B_k = the investment required to change the vector t_0 (link
    times with no project completed) into the vector t_k. B_k
    is the sum of all the costs b_{ij} that were incurred to
    change the travel time for a project link of the project
    combination k from t_{ij}^0 to t_{ij} $(t_{ij} < t_{ij}^0)$ where i, j are
    the connected nodes.

Equation 5.9 is the conservation equation (Kirchow I) for each
origin, with the objective function (minimization of total travel
time in system) defined by Equation 5.8. Since no capacity re-
straint is assumed, the solution of Equations 5.8 and 5.9 will
be a series of minimum-path trees for a particular network or
project combination which, assuming all-or-nothing loading,
assures that the total time spent in the system to satisfy the
given travel demands q_ℓ $(1 = 1, 2, \ldots,$ highest centroid number), will be minimized.

If different land use and traffic generation and distribution
patterns are to be studied, then a variety of different sets of
q_ℓ vectors (trip tables) will have to be used in Equation 5.9.

If n projects are contemplated, then the maximum number of
different combinations which might have to be studied is

$$\sum_{k=1}^{n} \binom{n}{k} = 2^n \tag{5.11}$$

Equation 5.11 indicates that in particular those combinations
of projects should be studied which provide that no equal or less
costly alternative can produce a greater benefit, i.e., lower
total time in the system.

Equations 5.8 to 5.11 assume that a single project link will
have two values, t_{ij}^0 and t_{ij}, and that if alternatives of the same
project are to be studied, then diverse values t_{ij}' requiring different investments b_{ij} can be used.

Generally, $t_{ij}' > t_{ij}''$ would imply $b_{ij}' < b_{ij}''$, since otherwise t_{ij}' would never be selected.

Ridley[5] suggests a linear dependence between investment and
link time for a particular project, i.e.,

$$k_{ij} = t_{ij} - a_{ij} \cdot b_{ij}; \quad t_{ij} \le k_{ij} \le t_{ij}^0 \tag{5.12}$$

where

t_{ij}^0 is the original upper-bound link time
(a very high number in the case of "new" links)

t_{ij} = the lower-bound link time

a_{ij} = benefit/unit investment for link (i,j)

b_{ij} = investment into project link (i,j)

The effect of investment into a single link can best be described graphically. For instance, Figures 5.11 and 5.13 show
the effect of increasing the investment into a single link (i,j).
The link time decreases in accordance with Figure 5.12, while
the effect on the total time in the system is indicated in Figure
5.13. At first the link did not belong to any shortest path (segment 0-1), but as the link time decreased, it began entering
into an increasing number of shortest path trees (segments 1-2,
2-3).

Due to the concave nature of the curve, it can be assumed
that in general, if any link is worth an investment, it should,
under the linearity assumption of Equation 5.12, receive the
maximum investment. Then only the lower-bound effects need

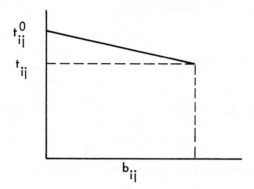

Figure 5. 12. Relationship between the investment and
travel time for a single link.

be studied. The network-evaluation procedure therefore assumes only two link times, one before a project is built (t_{ij}^0),
the other after it is built (t_{ij}).

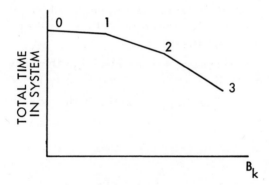

Figure 5. 13. Relationship between the total travel time
and investment into a link.

Appendix A

Project Tree Algorithm
(Single Project, Symmetric Network)

Input and Notation

Network N composed of nodes i, connected by links (i,j) having travel times (distances, costs) $t_{ij}(\geq 0)$; $t_{ij} = t_{ji}$. Associated with each node i are two numbers, t_i and s_i. The nodes i can be divided into complementary subsets X, $\overline{X}$, such that $N = X \cup \overline{X}$. The project link connects the nodes a and b.

Step 1. Initialization: Set $t_a = 0$; $s_a = 1$; $t_b = 0$, $s_b = 0$. All remaining $t_i = 999$ (high value), $s_i = 0$.
Assume all "reached" nodes $(t_i < 999)$ form a subset X, with the remaining nodes forming a complementary subset $\overline{X}$.

Step 2. Consider all links (i,j) connected the node(s) i that have been assigned to the set X in the preceding step to nodes $j \in \overline{X}$, and calculate values $t'_j = t_i + t_{ij}$; $s'_j = s_i + s_j$. Place the values t'_j, s'_j in a sequence table (table ordered by value t'_j).

Step 3. Select $Min(t'_j)$ from the sequence table. If $Min(t_j) < t_j$ go to Step 4, otherwise remove t'_j, s'_j from the sequence table and repeat Step 3.

Step 4. Set $t_j = t'_j$, $s_j = s'_j$ and reassign the node j from the set $\overline{X}$ to the set X.

Step 5. If the set $\overline{X}$ is empty, STOP. Otherwise return to Step 2.

Appendix B

NETWORK EVALUATOR

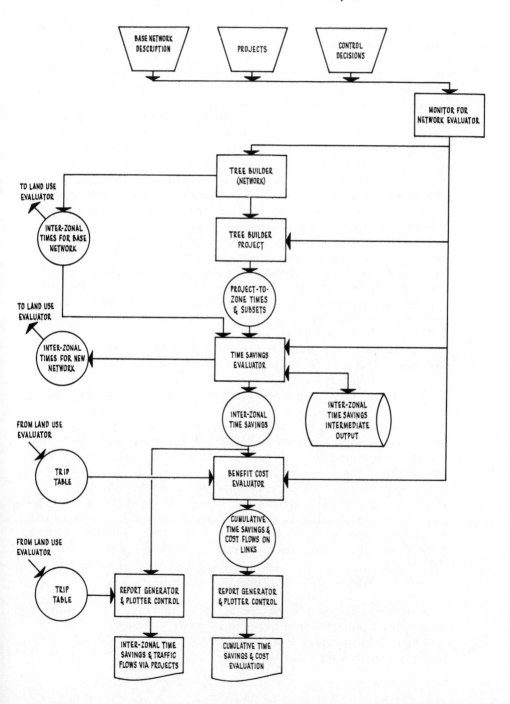

Appendix C

Quadratic Programming Interpretation of
the Project-Evaluation Problem

In many cases it may be advantageous to concentrate only on single and pairwise project interactions, especially if most of the higher-level effects prove to be negligible. The higher-level project combination effects which cannot be ignored can be taken into account by treating such combinations as separate "projects."

The following procedure, applicable to such cases, assumes that all project costs and single and pairwise project benefits have been determined, either in the manner described in the preceding Sections or by some other means. Except for the limitation with regard to higher-level interactions, it is a completely general method, applicable to a variety of problems where it is possible to evaluate the pairwise "benefits" of projects, procedures, data, or similar interacting categories.

In this procedure the positive or negative benefit values ($(n^2 + n)/2$ items) are used to form a triangularized benefit matrix M, whose diagonal elements (m_{ii}) represent the benefit of a project taken individually, and the remaining elements (m_{ij}, $i \neq j$) the mutual effect of the pairwise combinations of projects. The project costs can be taken into account in the form of a cost vector c.

The problem can now be stated as follows:
Determine $\delta^T M \delta$ and $c \cdot \delta$, subject to $\delta i = 0$ or 1, for various vectors δ, especially for such δ that $c \cdot \delta' > c \cdot \delta''$ implies $\delta'^T M \delta' \geq \delta''^T M \delta''$.

The vector δ is composed of elements δi. If project i belongs to a given project combination, then $\delta i = 1$, and $\delta i = 0$ if it does not. We are not generally interested in project combinations having a smaller benefit than some other project combination requiring less investment; this is indicated by the inequalities in the above equations.

A somewhat simplified version of the problem was posed by Kuhn[3] using a benefit matrix M' whose diagonal elements represent the net benefits of single projects ($m_{ii}-c_i$), where m_{ii} is the benefit of project i, and c_i its cost. His interest centered mainly on determining the maximum benefit project combination:

$$\text{Max } \delta^T M' \delta, \text{ subject to } \delta i = 0 \text{ or } 1$$

In order to obtain the matrix M' it is therefore necessary to determine a relationship between benefits and costs. For the transportation project-evaluation problem this would be a cost-to-time conversion ratio.

The difference between the project selection problem and Kuhn's problem may be best expressed graphically, as in Figure 5.14.

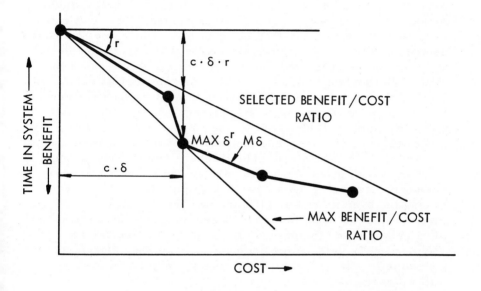

Figure 5.14. Various values on the project evaluation curve.

The selected benefit/cost ratio defines a line which passes through the origin (0 benefit, 0 cost). The objective in Kuhn's problem was to maximize the net benefit, as indicated in Figure 5.14. Another point of special interest on the benefit/cost curve was the point of tangency for a line drawn through the origin. The tangent will indicate the maximal benefit/cost ratio. This is also indicated in Figure 5.14.

In the present project-evaluation procedure both a benefit and a cost value is to be determined for any project combination, to define a point in the benefit/cost space, while in Kuhn's procedure only a single value (the net benefit) is sought.

If a logical computation procedure is used, at most two additive operations, with a partial sum and the total sum retained, are needed to determine the benefit (or net benefit) of any project combination, while, at most, one additive operation is needed to determine the project combination cost. This is independent of the number of projects (matrix size). As a rough estimate, it should be possible to generate the values for some

100,000 project combinations per second on a high-speed computer. The core requirements are small.

The procedure is indicated on a practical example in Table 5.2. It is based upon the determination of partial and total benefit sums and costs, and the retention of these values as long as needed, in a computation procedure in which increasingly larger project combinations are treated until all combinations which included the first project have been exhausted. The first row of the benefit matrix can then be ignored and the same procedure used on a diminished matrix, starting with the second project; the same is then repeated for the following projects on a constantly diminishing project matrix. The computation column in Table 5.2 shows that at most two additive operations are needed to determine the total and partial project benefits, the latter being the sum of all elements on the rows of all the projects of a particular combination and the column of the highest numbered project of the combination. The numbers refer to preceding total or partial project benefits, designated by their sequence numbers. As can be seen, they are required only for determining the benefits of the following project group, e.g., for all three project combinations that include project 1 only the results of calculations for the preceding two-project combinations are required. The demand for computer memory is, therefore, very small. The calculation of project combination cost is still simpler.

It should be mentioned that only those project combinations which meet some predetermined benefit/cost requirement need enter the output routine. The procedure therefore is not limited by the tape-writing speed of the computer.

Also, in case the simple additive property does not hold for project costs, then these can be treated in the same way as the project benefits.

The results for the given example have been plotted in Figure 5.15. The numbers refer to the sequence number of a project combination in the computation procedure. The optimal project combination and sequence in which the projects should be completed, in case investment possibilities are unlimited, is indicated.

Table 5.2. Computer Input and Results Abstracted for
Specific Example

	1	2	3	4
1	50	-10	-20	-10
2		20	20	0
3			30	-10
4				40

Benefit Matrix

30
10
20
20

Cost Vector

Seq. No.	Project Combination	Calculation Procedure	Partial Benefit	Total Benefit	Cost
		Total Benefit $\overbrace{}$ Partial Benefit $\underbrace{}$			
1	0		--	0	0
2	1		--	50	30
3	1, 2	$1 + m_{22} + m_{12}$	10	60	40
4	1, 3	$1 + m_{33} + m_{13}$	10	60	50
5	1, 4	$1 + m_{44} + m_{14}$	30	80	50
6	1, 2, 3	$3 + 4' + m_{23}$	30	90	60
7	1, 2, 4	$3 + 5' + m_{24}$	30	90	60
8	1, 3, 4	$4 + 5' + m_{34}$	20	80	70
9	1, 2, 3, 4	$6 + 7' + m_{34}$	20	110	80
10	2	--	--	20	10
11	2, 3	$10 + m_{33} + m_{23}$	50	70	30
12	2, 4	$10 + m_{44} + m_{24}$	40	60	30
13	2, 3, 4	$11 + 12' + m_{34}$	30	100	50
14	3	--	--	30	20
15	3, 4	$14 + m_{44} + m_{34}$	30	60	40
16	4	--	--	40	20

Output

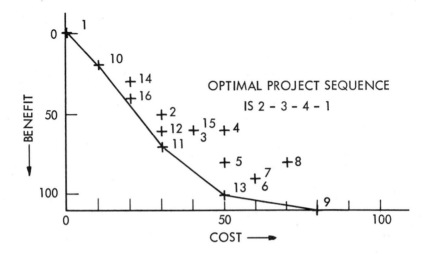

Figure 5.15. Benefits and costs of projects plotted from
Table 5.2.

Properties of the Benefit Matrix

1. For any benefit matrix M there exists a complementary
matrix M^c with the following property:

$$\delta^T M \delta = K + \gamma^T M^c \gamma, \quad \delta_i, \gamma_i = 0 \text{ or } 1, \quad \delta_i + \gamma_i = 1 \quad (5.13)$$

K is the sum of all elements in the matrix M.

Equation 5.13 indicates that for any benefit matrix M there
exists another matrix M^c from which it is possible to obtain the
benefit of a project combination by concentrating on the projects
that do not belong to it.   This is useful in case it is desired to
determine the benefits of project combinations, starting with
all projects "in, " as for instance in a "branch and bound" type
approach, as suggested in Ford,[1] or when values for only the
higher investment region are desired.

The off-diagonal elements of the M^c matrix are the same as
those of the M matrix, while the diagonal elements M_{ii}^c are
the negative sum of all elements in a particular row and column
of the matrix

$$M(M_{ii}^c = -\sum_{j \geq i} M_{ij} - \sum_{j < i} M_{ji}).$$

The proof of Equation 5.13 is trivial.

Example: For the matrix M used in the preceding example:

	1	2	3	4
1	50	-10	-20	-10
2		20	20	0
3			30	-10
4				40

The complementary matrix M^c is:

	1	2	3	4
1	-10	-10	-20	-10
2		-30	20	0
3			-20	-10
4				-20

The sum of all elements in the original matrix is K = 110, for $\delta = (1, 0, 1, 1)$ then $\gamma = (0, 1, 0, 0)$, and

$$\delta^T M \delta = 80 \quad \text{while} \quad K - \gamma^T M^c \gamma = 110 - 30 = 80,$$

i.e., both values are the same.

2. For any benefit matrix M there exists a matrix N with the property that

$$\delta^T M \delta = (1 - \delta)^T N \delta \tag{5.14}$$

The expression on the right-hand side of Equation 5.14 can be interpreted as the "cut" value of a network, i.e., the sum of the values on arcs (lengths, capacities) that separate a subset of network nodes from the complementary node subset. It can be proved that $M = E^T N E$, where E is the incidence matrix of a network.

Example:

N:	1	2	3	4
1	--	1	3	4
2		--	2	4
3			--	3
4				--

$M = E^T NE$:

	1	2	3	4
1	8	-2	-6	-8
2		7	-4	-8
3			8	-6
4				11

As can be seen from the example, one matrix can be very easily generated from the other. For instance, the "network" matrix N can be converted to the "benefit" matrix M by taking the negative of twice the value for the off-diagonal elements and the sum of all values on each particular row and column for the diagonal elements.

In the given example the minimal cut in the network N is the one that separates node 2 from nodes 1, 3, 4; its value is 7. The same value can be obtained as the benefit of "project" combinations 2 and also 1, 3, 4 for the benefit matrix M. Similarly, the maximal cut in matrix N is the one that separates nodes 1, 2 from nodes 3, 4; its value is 13. The same value is obtained as the benefit of "project" combinations 1, 2 and also 3, 4.

The above identity makes it possible to utilize network algorithms to obtain specific project benefit values, and vice versa. It must be mentioned that most network algorithms apply to positive-link values only; the project matrix approach therefore appears to be more general, but limited to symmetric networks.

3. In the special case of benefit matrices where the benefit for a project combination is assumed to be the sum of the benefits of all projects in the combination $(\delta^T M\delta)$ minus the benefits of all projects not in the combination $[(1 - \delta)^T M(1 - \delta)]$, the benefit value can be easily determined by computing a benefit vector b composed of b_i elements, where

$$b_i = \frac{(\sum_{j=1}^{n} M_{ij} + \sum_{j=1}^{n} M_{ij})}{2} \tag{5.15}$$

Then

$$\delta^T M\delta - [(1 - \delta)^T M(1 - \delta)] = b \cdot \gamma \tag{5.16}$$

where

$$\gamma_i = 2\delta_i - 1 \tag{5.17}$$

Expression 5.17 produces a vector γ such that

$$\gamma_i = 1 \quad \text{if } \delta_i = 1, \quad \text{and } \gamma_i = -1 \text{ if } \delta_i = 0.$$

Example: For the benefit matrix:

	1	2	3	4
1	50	-10	-20	-10
2		20	20	0
3			30	-10
4				40

the vector b is: (30, 25, 25, 30).

In case projects 1, 4 are assumed "in" and projects 2, 3 "out," then δ = (1, 0, 0, 1) and γ = (1, -1, -1, 1) and expression 9 will hold, since:

$\delta^T M \delta$	80
$-(1 - \delta)^T M (1 - \delta)$	$\underline{-70}$
$= \quad b \cdot \gamma$	$= 10$

References

1. Ford, L. R. , and D. R. Fulkerson, <u>Flows in Networks</u>, Princeton University Press, Princeton, New Jersey, 1962.

2. Fratar, T. J. , "Vehicular Trip Distribution by Successive Approximations," <u>Traffic Quarterly</u>, <u>8</u>, No. 1, 53-65 (January, 1954).

3. Kuhn, T. E. , <u>Public Enterprise Economics and Transport Problem</u>, 92-98, University of California Press, Berkeley, California, 1962.

4. Loubal, P. S. , "Project Selection and Coordination in Transportation Planning," Bay Area Transportation Study Commission, January, 1966.

5. Ridley, T. M. , "An Investment Policy to Reduce the Travel Time in a Transportation Network," Operations Research Center, University of California, Berkeley, California, December, 1965.

6. Traffic Assignment Manual, U. S. Department of Commerce,
   Bureau of Public Roads, June, 1964.

7. Weingartner, H. M., "Capital Budgeting of Interrelated
   Projects: Survey and Synthesis," Management Science,
   12, No. 7, 485-516 (March, 1966).

Chapter 6

OPERATIONS RESEARCH IN MEDICAL AND HOSPITAL PRACTICE

William J. Horvath

6.1 Variable Demands for Services in Hospitals

Introduction. A hospital administrator has to deal with many
vexatious problems in the course of his daily activities, but
none are more persistent or ubiquitous than those caused by
the fluctuating demand for services. This demand is governed
by chance factors which, in many instances, can be described
by a simple Poisson process, in which the occurrence of an
event is independent of the number of previous occurrences and
the time since the last occurrence. As a consequence, facilities and staff needed to deal with this demand must be capable
of handling loads far in excess of the average in order to reduce
the probability of overload to some acceptable low level. Facilities designed for high peak-loads will be underutilized, and
therefore inefficient, a high percentage of the time. In the
hospital field, bed occupancy, the percentage of time that hospital beds have patients assigned to them, is a commonly used
measure of efficient operation. The goal of the hospital administrator is to keep this figure as high and as constant as possible in the face of a varying need.

While the economic pressures for high utilization tend to keep
the operating level near capacity, the consequent increase in
overload situations may have even more serious repercussions.
The usual method of dealing with overload in noncritical situations, queuing, is not a satisfactory solution for emergency
medical cases. Even in the outpatient department, where the
medical situation is not critical, excessive waiting times add
to the anxiety of the patient and therefore have medical consequences in addition to any economic losses incurred.

Because of the obvious importance and urgency of this problem, it has received the attention of a number of operations
research teams working in hospitals. One of the earliest
groups in the hospital field, that headed by Professor Charles
Flagle of the School of Hygiene and Public Health of the Johns
Hopkins University, has been studying operational problems at
the Johns Hopkins Hospital since 1956.[7] Many of their studies
have been concerned with the effects of fluctuating demand on

hospital services, and, since they present particularly good
examples of research in this field, some of their work will be
discussed below.

A Study of Bed Occupancy at the Johns Hopkins Hospital. The
problems involved in studying bed occupancy, or the inpatient
hospital census, have been discussed in some detail in a mono-
graph by Dr. John Young of Johns Hopkins, and the author is
indebted to Dr. Young for permission to use some of the material from this publication.[8] A preliminary examination of the
Johns Hopkins Hospital records was used to gain some idea of
the magnitude of the inpatient hospital census. Figure 6. 1
shows the monthly average census of the hospital over a six-
year period. On the same chart there are superimposed scaled-
down figures for the hospital census of the City of Baltimore and
the entire U. S. hospital census. The three sets of curves exhibit a certain amount of synchrony and indicate some seasonal
effects on the variation in the hospital population. It is sufficient here to note that variations of the order of 10 per cent to
15 per cent in the number of beds occupied in a 1,000-bed hospital are not unusual even in monthly averages. The daily
fluctuations, which are the immediate concern of the administrator, tend to be somewhat larger.

In attempting to identify the factors that influence the rise
and fall in the hospital census, it soon became apparent that
the two factors which contributed to the census, the admission
rate and the length of stay, were both chance variables and
that the mathematics of stochastic processes could describe
quite accurately the observed variation. For example, several
investigators[1,2,6] have shown that the number of admissions per
day could be described by the Poisson distribution

$$P_n = \frac{e^{-\lambda}\lambda^n}{n!} \tag{6.1}$$

where P_n is the proportion of days with 0, 1, 2, 3, etc., admissions and λ is the average admission rate. This a well-
known function in accident statistics; it indicates that the risk
of hospitalization in the population is constant in time and is
identical for all individuals. In addition, the probability of
occurrence is independent of the time since the last occurrence.
Obviously, these conditions would not hold in the event of large
catastrophes or epidemics, but they seem to be in accord with
the every-day experience of hospital admitting rooms.

The second factor contributing to the fluctuation in hospital
census is the frequency distribution of the length of stay.
Figure 6.2 shows a compilation of statistics from four wards
at the Johns Hopkins Hospital. The curve has a peak at about

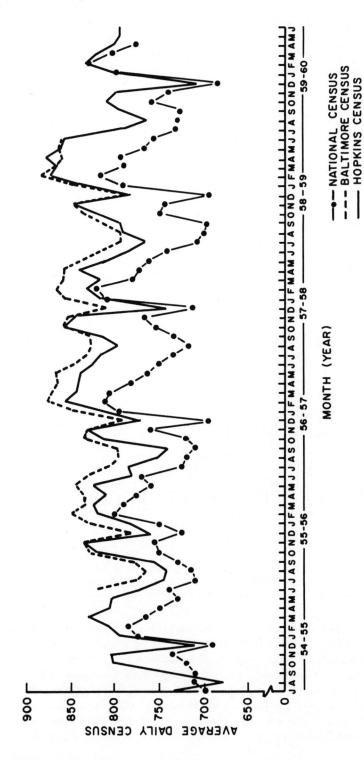

Figure 6.1. Fluctuation of hospital population. [2]

six to eight days and then descends in a long tail. According to
Young,[8] most of these curves can be fitted by a gamma function.
A smooth curve described by this function has been drawn
through the observed points in Figure 6.2. The equation for
this function is

$$f(t) = \frac{a^r}{\Gamma(r)} t^{r-1} e^{-at} \qquad\qquad (6.2)$$

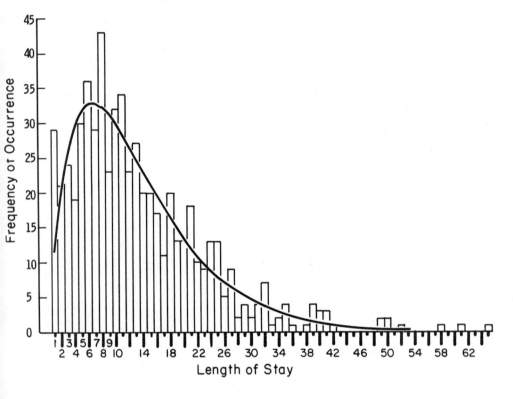

Figure 6.2. Frequency distribution of length of stay for ward patients, the
Johns Hopkins Hospital, Osler 2, 3, 4, 6; Oct. 1960 to Feb.
1961.[2]

It has two constants, a and r, which can be determined from
the data. The proportion of lengths of stay, $f(t)$, which last a
given time, t, can then be determined from Equation 6.2. With
the aid of these two equations, it is now possible to determine
the percentage of time that the hospital census exceeds any particular level, given the observed values of λ, a, and r.

Although the use of a mathematical model of a process, as
exemplified here, can be very helpful in many operational

decisions -- for example, one can use it to design a bed capacity which would be adequate in a specified high percentage of the time (say 99%) -- it merely accepts the random nature of the events without trying to control them.   The Johns Hopkins study went beyond this by noting that admissions could be separated into two groups, those which were unscheduled (or emergency cases) and those in which the admission was scheduled ahead of time (and therefore could be deferred if necessary).   They proposed, therefore, to exert a control over the fluctuations by using a call list of scheduled admissions and admit enough persons each day in this category to bring the system up to some predetermined occupancy level, B, allowing enough leeway to take care of the expected unscheduled admissions.   Figure 6.3 shows a schematic diagram of this process where a 25-bed level is maintained in a 30-bed ward by means of the call list. For example, if the census drops to 20 beds at a particular time, five persons are scheduled for the next day to bring the level up to 25.

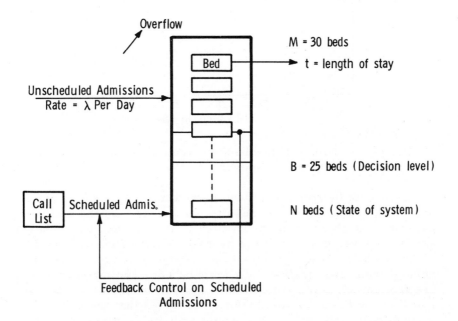

Figure 6.3. Feedback control model of a hospital ward. [2]

The calculations for this feedback process are somewhat complicated and may be found in Reference 8.   The results are shown in Figures 6.4 and 6.5.   The first of these shows the average census for different decision levels, and the second shows the probability that a patient may have to be turned away

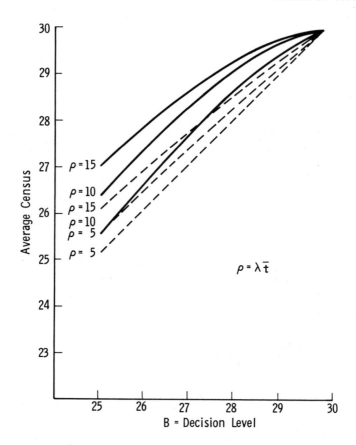

Figure 6.4. Effect of feedback control on census, the Johns
Hopkins Hospital. [2]

(or dealt with by some overflow method) under the assumed
operating conditions. The results, of course, depend on the
parameter ρ which is the product of λ, the average unscheduled
admissions per day, and $\bar{t}$ the average length of stay. Two sets
of curves are given in Figure 6.4; the dotted curves were calculated from the equations of queuing theory and the solid curves
are from a computer simulation. The difference is due to the
fact that the theoretical calculation assumes that the beds are
immediately filled up as they become available provided that
the patient arrives within the next 24 hours, while the computer
results allow for the fact that census counts are taken at midnight and discharges occur in the morning. The true value of
the average census probably lies somewhere between these.

The conclusion of these studies was that the fluctuation in
occupancy under feedback control was much less than under the
present system. But, obviously, there will still be some over-

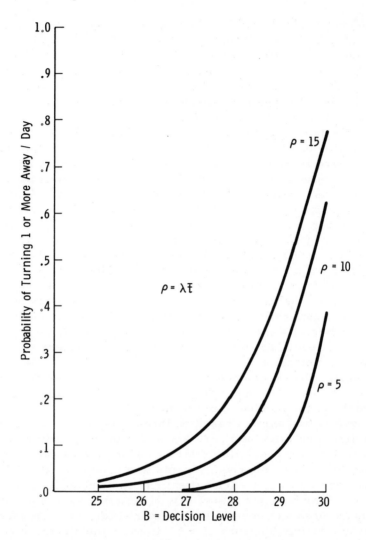

Figure 6.5. Effect of feedback control on overload, the Johns
Hopkins Hospital. [2]

flow, and the optimum decision level will have to be determined
from the relative costs of low occupancy levels as compared
with high overflow. Decisions of this nature are always being
made in the medical profession but not always consciously.
This formal mathematical model gives a quantitative basis for
determining the policy. Further studies are underway on this
system with the eventual objective of providing the admissions
officer with a daily computer output showing the B level, the
expected overflow, patients to be scheduled for each of the
patient areas in the hospital, etc. The decision rules could

then be adjusted empirically to keep the bed occupancy at reasonably high level without excessive overflow. Optimum rules, based on statistical decision theory, could be derived if the relative costs in monetary, or other terms, were available of underutilization versus overflow. This could be done once specific plans for dealing with overflow are made and suggests a fertile field for further research.

A Study of Nursing Requirements. Staff requirements are also affected by variable demand for services. If the staffing of a ward is based on some average level of occupancy, there will be peak activity periods when the nursing staff cannot cope with patient demand. If, on the other hand, staff requirements are based on peak activity levels, the ward will be overstaffed a high percentage of the time, and therefore inefficiently run. One way of coping with these fluctuations is to keep a basic staff on each ward to handle the average load and then have available a supplementary staff to be assigned daily to those areas with predictable overload. Nursing requirements, however, must be based not only on numbers of patients but also on individual patient needs, which are also highly variable. Accordingly, a method of classifying patients by their relative nursing needs has to be developed before a system such as this can be implemented.

Again, the experience of the Johns Hopkins Hospital Operations Research Group is highly relevant and will be used to illustrate the method of procedure. They developed a patient classification system based on three categories, self-care, partial care, and total care according to the condition of the patient.[4,6] A check list of factors describing a patient's needs in terms of nursing requirements was used to determine the category into which each patient had to be placed. Once this system had been put into effect, a sampling survey of the total amount of direct bedside care required for each category of patient during the hours of 6 A.M. to 12 midnight was conducted. The results of this survey are shown in Figure 6.6. There is a distribution about a mean value for each classification, the means being approximately one half hour for a self-care patient, one hour for a partial-care patient, and two and one half hours for a total-care patient. A typical illustration of how nursing need fluctuates in a particular ward may be seen in Figure 6.7, which shows the variation in the percentage of patients in the total-care category in a single 29-bed ward over an eight-month period. Comparative curves for the number of total-care patients in four identical wards of the hospital are shown in Figure 6.8. Activity in the four wards seems to be completely uncorrelated, indicating that the suggestion for meeting increased demands on a particular ward by shifting supplementary personnel should be feasible.

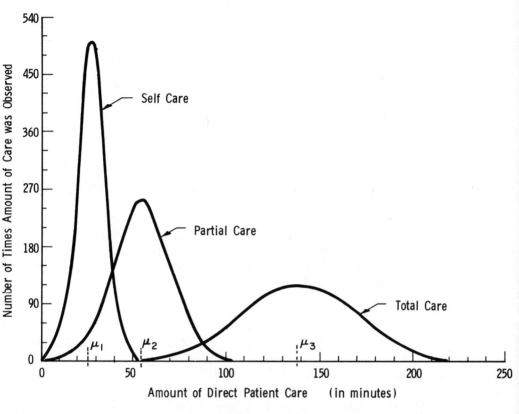

Figure 6.6. Frequency distributions of direct patient care, 6 A.M. to 12 A.M., the Johns Hopkins Hospital.

In order to implement this procedure, the charge nurse on each floor places check marks on a daily form listing all the ward patients. These indicate each individual's need for care according to the predetermined list of factors. The number of patients in each category can then be determined from this chart. The nursing supervisor then determines her nursing requirements for the following day by computing the number of hours of direct nursing care required on each ward, adding a factor for "other" nursing duties which were determined to be 20 hours per eight-hour shift for a typical 29-30-bed nursing unit. As described here, the procedure has been reduced to a simple bookkeeping operation. In actual practice the addition or removal of nursing personnel is still based to a large extent on the experience and judgment of the nursing supervisor and depends on her familiarity with the particular skills needed on each floor, type of nursing effort, etc. However, the system as outlined here offers a logical method of procedure which can be modified to suit individual needs.

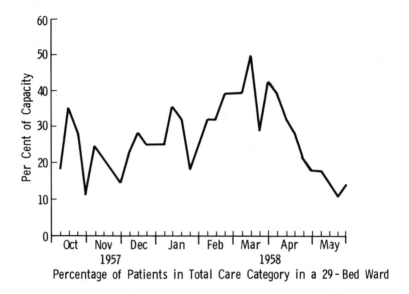

Percentage of Patients in Total Care Category in a 29-Bed Ward

Figure 6.7. Percentage of patients in total care category for
typical medical ward, the Johns Hopkins Hospital.

As an interesting sidelight on this research, Barr[3] at the
Oxford Regional Hospital Board in England carried out a similar
study of a three-category patient classification system. Despite
the fact that his definitions differ somewhat from the Hopkins
group, the ratio of the nursing time required for the three care
groups was 1:2:5, exactly the same as in the Hopkins study.
Figures 6.9, 6.10, and 6.11 are from Barr's report and show
the frequency distribution curve for the workload in nine hospital
wards in terms of work units (one unit is the time devoted to one
self-care patient per day), the fluctuation in workload for a
female surgical ward, and the effect on the workload fluctuation
of combining two wards (sharing nursing personnel). Barr points
out that since the fluctuations are approximately equal and independent, the variance of a combined ward will be the root mean
square of the individual variances, while if they are operated
independently it will be their sum. This implies that the mean
fluctuation in workload as measured by the variance would be
reduced about 30 per cent by combining the personnel and patients
of two identical wards. The actual data for the two wards studied in Figure 6.11 shows that a significant reduction in the fluctuation in workload could have been achieved by combining the
two wards observed. Measured at the 95 per cent confidence
level, the reduction amounts to slightly less than 10 per cent.
The approach used in the Johns Hopkins study is, of course,
more drastic and, in principle, more efficient since they redis-
tribute the workforce over many wards based on forecast needs.

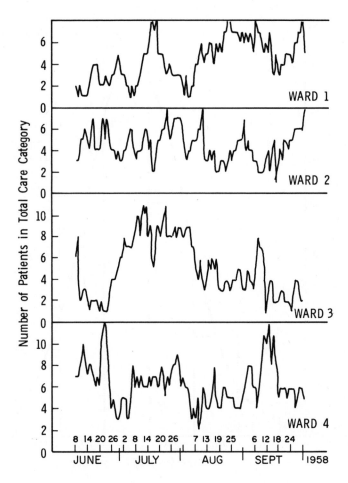

Figure 6.8. Comparison of total care patients in four typical
medical wards, the Johns Hopkins Hospital.

It is nevertheless interesting to note the close agreement between the two groups on the relative nursing workload for the
three patient categories, despite the fact that procedures and
definitions of patient needs differ somewhat in the two systems.
This suggests that the results of individual hospital studies are
capable of wide generalization.

The Simulation of Hospital Operations by Computer Programs.
The two previous examples of how operations research can help
administrators cope with the problem of variable demand for
hospital services have dealt with studies conducted by a group
acting in a staff capacity to the executive in charge of the hospital. As a consequence, the studies were oriented toward a
particular problem in a specific hospital. The results, therefore, were especially valuable to that hospital, although as

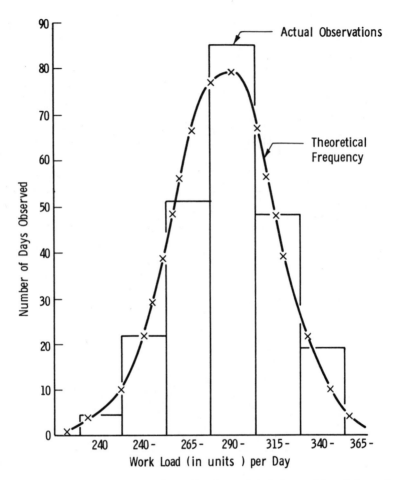

Figure 6.9. Frequency distribution of total workload for nine
wards over 230 days, Oxford R. H. B.

indicated in the last example, the approach is perfectly general
and the findings can be applied with little or no modification to
other hospitals as well.

Another, and more general, approach is possible. This is
to focus attention on the problem without reference to any specific hospital and to formulate a model in such general terms
that it can be applied to a wide variety of situations. This
approach has both advantages and disadvantages. It is usually
carried out in an academic setting, and is therefore not subject
to the pressures which come from the executive to research
groups on the staff. On the other hand, the research worker,
being far removed from an operating organization, will miss
the satisfaction of seeing the implementation of his studies in
actual operation. An even more severe drawback is that the

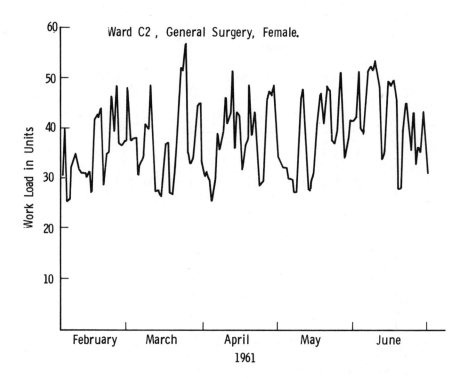

Figure 6.10. Fluctuation of workload, Oxford R. H. B.

models arrived at in the academic atmosphere are sometimes
so far removed from reality that there is not just the question
of finding someone to use them but, in fact, they cannot be used
at all. The work which will be discussed below fortunately does
not suffer from this criticism and reflects the practical orientation of its authors.

Of the multitude of models which can be used to represent
operational situations, the most direct is the step-by-step
simulation on a digital computer of a well-understood and carefully documented procedure. Such a program has been written
by Fetter and Thompson[5] to study bed utilization in a maternity
hospital. Their program, written in SIMSCRIPT, is based on
observed distributions of labor, delivery, and post-partum re-
covery time, and the known Poisson distribution of admissions.
They have validated the program by comparing its predictions
with the actual operating statistics of the Grace-New Haven
Community Hospital which was used as their data base. Table
6.1 shows the occupancy ratio for the post-partum and delivery
rooms for 308 actual operating days compared with a simulation
run from the computer. There is very close agreement between
the two sets of data and both of them fit the Poisson distribution
mentioned earlier.

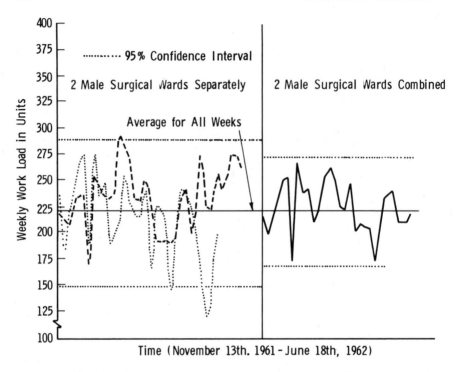

Figure 6.11. Effect of combining two wards on fluctuation of workload, Oxford R. H. B.

The value of a working simulation model is that once it has been perfected to the point where it accurately represents the actual operation, it may be used to run experiments to determine how the operation would change under different policies or different conditions. For example, it would be interesting to find out how the occupancy changes with patient load. Table 6.2 shows the data for the present load of 1320 patients per year compared with a 15 per cent decrease (1130) and a 25 per cent increase (1660). Information of this sort is of considerable value for long-range planning.

A valid computer model can also be used to simulate changes in operating policy. For example, a study of the effect of scheduling deliveries on the operation of this particular hospital was also simulated. Deliveries can be scheduled by using drugs to induce labor prior to the expected natural delivery date. They are done both for the convenience of the patient and of the obstetrician who might prefer a particular time or date for the birth. The hospital under study did not use this system, but data on the processing times of patients using elective induction of labor were obtained from another hospital in which this procedure was in use. The elective induction policy tested in this

Table 6.1. Comparison of Occupancy Statistics,
Hospital vs. Model[5]

No. of rooms	Proportion of total time given number of rooms was occupied			
	Post-partum		Delivery	
	Hospital	Model	Hospital	Model
0	0.4788	0.4510	0.6118	0.6209
1	0.3410	0.3496	0.2983	0.2882
2	0.1264	0.1460	0.0802	0.0759
3	0.0385	0.0423	0.0069	0.0130
4	0.0129	0.0097	0.0024	0.0018
5	0.0024	0.0012	0.0004	0.0002
6	0.0000	0.0002		
Mean No. of rooms	0.7809	0.8147	0.4912	0.4873
Std. dev.	0.862	0.916	0.499	0.501

experiment was to allow admissions twice per day with a maximum of seven patients per admission. Tables 6.3 and 6.4 show the results of this simulation. There is a small increase in the utilization of the labor and delivery rooms and a corresponding decrease in bed utilization. However, the latter was deemed not significant and there is no reduction in bed requirements for either the 99 per cent or 95 per cent service level (1 per cent and 5 per cent overflow). One of the factors limiting the effectiveness of an elective admission policy in obstetrical cases is that, unlike the corresponding situation in general hospitals, elective admissions to a maternity ward still have to be processed in a very narrow time interval near the expected birth date of the child. The use of a call list based on occupancy feedback data such as proposed in the Johns Hopkins study would be much more difficult to implement and has not been examined in this setting.

These are just two examples of the sorts of experiments that can be carried out with a simulation model on a computer. Fetter and Thompson[5] have already experimented with the simulation of surgical wards and outpatient clinics and are planning to use simulation models in other areas of hospital

Table 6.2. Effect of Increasing Load on Facility Utilization[5]

Facilities Available	Patients/Year								
	1130			1320			1660		
	Utilization	Mean No. Used	Std. Dev. of Usage	Utilization	Mean No. Used	Std. Dev. of Usage	Utilization	Mean No. Used	Std. Dev. of Usage
Labor (5 beds)	0.1763	0.8816	0.9486	0.2042	1.0210	1.0215	0.2596	1.2982	1.1249
Reg. Del. (2 rooms)	0.0572	0.1144	0.3371	0.0683	0.1365	0.3695	0.0869	0.1738	0.4150
C. Del. (1 room)	0.0196	0.0196	0.1387	0.0220	0.0220	0.1467	0.0240	0.0240	0.1532
P. P. (5 beds)	0.0313	0.1567	0.4002	0.0369	0.1844	0.4351	0.0463	0.2316	0.4870
Beds (25 beds)	0.5107	12.7671	3.4956	0.5929	14.8222	3.7391	0.7359	18.3798	3.7707
Beds req'd for given service level	0.99	21 beds		23 beds			>25 beds		
	0.95	19 beds		21 beds			>25 beds		
	0.90	17 beds		20 beds			24 beds		

Table 6.3. Occupancy Statistics for Various Proportions of Elective Inductions[5]

| Number of Units Provided | Per Cent of Patients Who Are Elective Inductions | | | | | | | | |
| | 0 | | | 10 | | | 20 | | |
	Utilization	Mean No. Used	Std. Dev. of Usage	Utilization	Mean No. Used	Std. Dev. of Usage	Utilization	Mean No. Used	Std. Dev. of Usage
Labor	0.2953	4.4298	2.3783	0.3112	4.6682	2.3782	0.3276	4.9135	2.3784
Reg. Del.	0.0975	0.4873	0.8396	0.1083	0.5417	0.8406	0.1227	0.6136	0.8409
C. Del.	0.0771	0.0771	0.2972	0.0647	0.0647	0.2105	0.0586	0.0586	0.2103
P. P.	0.0543	0.8147	0.8411	0.0559	0.8391	0.8412	0.0574	0.8605	0.8413
Beds	0.7450	74.4971	9.5159	0.7324	73.2363	9.5215	0.7281	72.8117	9.5191

Table 6.4. Facility Requirements for Elective Induction Policy[5]

| Facility Type | Required Service Level | No. of Units Required at Given Per Cent Elective Induction | | |
		0	10	20
Labor	0.99	10 (0.986)	11 (0.988)	11 (0.991)
Reg. Del.	0.99	3 (0.998)	3 (0.996)	3 (0.995)
C. Del.	0.99	1	1	1
P. P.	0.99	3 (0.989)	3 (0.987)	3 (0.987)
Beds	0.99	96	96	96
Beds	0.95	89	89	89

and public health work. Computer simulation, if based on a
sound empirical understanding of actual operating conditions,
can provide administrators and planners with a basic tool for
decision making in the hospital field.

Summary and Conclusions. This Section has presented just
a few examples of how hospital administrators can cope with
some of the problems resulting from the uneven demand for
services. This is a most fruitful area for operations research,
since the need for such studies will increase with time as the
rising costs of medical care exert even greater pressure on
the hospitals and health system for greater efficiency.

6.2 The Role of Operations Research in the Study of Medical Diagnosis

Introduction. Large organizations have many common operating features which are independent of the specific purposes of
the organization. This fact greatly simplifies the problems
faced by an operations research worker entering a new field.
By identifying problems in the new area which are common to
those in organizations previously studied, he can apply some
of the solutions already available to the problems at hand. It
is not surprising, therefore, that the earliest applications of
operations research in the health field dealt with such matters
as queuing of patients entering hospitals, automated data processing, nursing work loads, maintenance of adequate levels
of medical supplies in hospitals, and studies of the cost of

services and equipment. These are all familiar problems to
the operations research worker, although in applying the results of previous studies to the medical field he necessarily
had to modify them in conformity with the special requirements
of this particular area.

Thorough familiarization with the special requirements of a
new field is standard procedure for all operations research
workers. For by this means they will not only uncover problems which will yield to standard techniques in their repertoire,
but they will also find problems which are unique to a single
area or profession. In the practice of medicine, the physician
has such a unique role. He is not only responsible for the medical treatment of his patients, but must strive to maintain an
attitude of complete impartiality and confidentiality in his deal-
ings with them. From the information gained in his preliminary
interview and subsequent examination of his patient, he must
make a diagnosis of the illness and then prescribe an appropriate
treatment. While it is generally recognized that effective treat-
ments do not exist for all diseases, so that unreasonable expec-
tations of rapid cure are not held by the average patient, the
diagnostic function of the physician is less well understood and
seldom questioned. In recent years, the rapid growth of new
knowledge in the medical field has caused considerable concern
with the ability of the average physician to keep pace with this
knowledge and, in this connection, some consideration has been
given to helping the physician overcome the limitations inherent
in the diagnostic process by providing some sort of computer-
aided diagnostic system.

The process of diagnosis is really not unique to the medical
field. A skilled garage mechanic or television repairman faces
the same sort of problem in trying to locate a specific fault in
a mechanical or electronic system as the physician does in determining the specific cause of ill health. Many companies in
the equipment-maintenance field have constructed flow charts
for the location of faults in complex electrical systems, based
on voltage measurements and other indications at certain test
points. About eight years ago, Ledley and Lusted[12] proposed
a similar systematic approach to medical diagnosis. By starting with the symptom complex presented by the patient, they
propose to arrive at the correct diagnosis through the application
of symbolic logic to the total corpus of medical knowledge. Since
the operations of symbolic logic lend themselves to programming
on the digital computer, the Ledley-Lusted paper and subsequent
studies have given rise to the hope that computer-aided medical
diagnosis can become a practical reality.

The difficulty in implementing this scheme lies in the well-
known fact that logical relations in medicine are not all-or-nothing

propositions. If a patient has a certain disease, there is only
a certain probability that he will have a particular sign or symptom. These specific probabilities are rarely, if ever, known
and discussions of the subject in medical textbooks rely on terms
such as "seldom" or "frequently," rather than exact numerical
probabilities. In fact, as Ledley and Lusted point out, these
probabilities may not be constant, but assume different values
as diagnostic tests are improved or population characteristics
are altered.

The collection of meaningful data on the probability of occurrence of specific signs and symptoms for the different disease
states is therefore a necessary prelude to any form of computer-
aided diagnosis. Computers may, of course, be used to collect
such data by codifying medical record-keeping, so that clinical
material would be more readily available for analysis; but the
immediate need is for research on the raw materials of medical
diagnosis, not the automation of an imperfect and poorly understood process. Such research calls for the combined ingenuity
of operations research workers, with their techniques for ex-
tracting meaningful relations from operational data, and of
physicians active in clinical practice who have the necessary
experience and background in the application of medical knowledge.

Some indication of how this research can be carried out may
be found in the results of recent studies on screening for chronic
diseases. The purpose of such screening procedures is to find
cases of a specific disease in persons who are not yet under
treatment, at a time when the disease process is minimal and
may possibly be halted before it leads to a fatal outcome. What
is usually involved is a test or group of tests applied to a population of individuals, who may or may not have symptoms, to
determine if they have some particular disease. The interest
is usually in the so-called "silent" diseases, such as diabetes,
cancer, hypertension, and a number of similar ailments which
in the long run could be fatal but present no serious symptoms
requiring medical attention in their early stages. Two examples
of studies of the results of such screening tests are discussed
below.

The Cytological Screening for Cervical Cancer. A simple
test for cancer of the cervix involves collecting exfoliated cells
from the female genital tract and transferring them to a microscope slide for staining and examination by a cytologist. Known
as the Papanicolaou smear test, after its originator, the test is
widely used by gynecologists and obstetricians in their routine
practice. The popularization of cancer "check-up" tests in
recent years has resulted in a particularly heavy load of such
material on the rather limited facilities available for cytological

diagnosis. Accordingly, the American Cancer Society and the
National Cancer Institute contracted for a project at the Air-
borne Instrument Laboratories of the Cutler-Hammer Company
to study the possibility of automatic screening of Papanicolaou
smears with electronic equipment. [14] In addition to constructing
an automatic scanning microscope to record and store data from
the slides, the research group undertook a quantitative evaluation of the diagnostic criteria used by the cytologist in determining whether a slide containing cells from a particular patient
was either positive or negative for cancer. Without such a study,
it would not have been possible to design automatic screening
equipment, since the success of such equipment depended on
simulating the performance of the cytologist. However, at the
same time, the necessity of expressing the judgments of the
cytologist in numerically measurable terms offered a rare opportunity to evaluate the effectiveness of this particular diagnostic procedure.

Accordingly, an extensive measurement program was undertaken to establish quantitatively the criteria used by the cytologist to determine malignancy. Over 700 microscope slides of
cell specimens taken in routine clinical practice from about
500 women (some had more than one smear taken) were used.
The slides were divided into two groups: (1) a random sample
of smears from normal patients with no evidence of malignancy,
and (2) smears taken from patients in whom cervical cancer
had been confirmed by biopsy or other surgical methods. Early
in the study it was determined that the primary measurable criterion used by the cytologist to detect the presence of cancer of
the cervix was the percentage of cells with large, dense nuclei.
On the basis of these results, a number of tentative criteria for
suspicious cells, expressed in measurable units of size and
density, were derived and the screening effectiveness of each
criterion or combination of criteria was determined. [10]

The analysis showed that regardless of how the criteria were
chosen, there were always some smears from confirmed cancer
patients which showed very few cells exceeding the chosen criterion, while the smears from some normal patients had more
than this number of cells. In effect, therefore, the two population groups overlapped with respect to the chosen criterion used
to indicate the presence of cancer. Thus, an inevitable consequence of this particular diagnostic process is that, wherever
the criterion is set, some persons who do not have the disease
will be classified as having it (false positives) and some who do
have the disease will be classified as not having it (false negatives). As the criterion is made more stringent, we can decrease the number of false negatives, but only at the expense
of increasing the number of false positives. A numerical

example taken from the actual data will serve to illustrate the
magnitude of this effect.

Data for the two population groups, the normals (true negatives) and the confirmed cancer patients (true positives), were
plotted separately to show the distribution of percentage of
smears containing a given fraction of suspicious cells. These
distribution curves were highly skewed, but in most cases a
good fit could be obtained with a logarithmic normal function.
Figure 6.12 shows two cumulative distribution curves, which
had been fitted to the actual data, plotted on a logarithmic

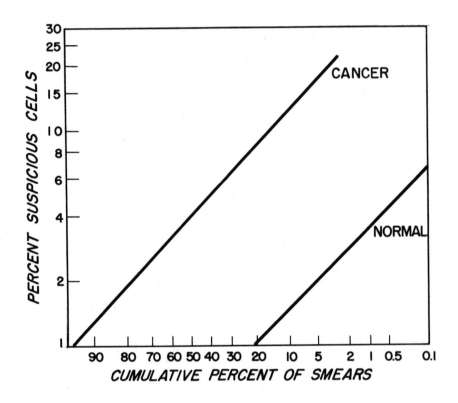

Figure 6.12. Cumulative distribution curves of percentage of
              smears on which the percentage of suspicious
              cells (d ≥ 10μ, ε > 0.5) exceeds a given number.

probability scale for a normal and a cancer population, using
as cell-selection criteria a nuclear diameter of 10 microns or
greater and an optical extinction coefficient exceeding 0.5.
These curves show that if we required at least 2 per cent of
the cells on the smear to exceed these criteria of nuclear size
and density, we would miss 22 per cent of the cancer patients

(false negatives) and would classify 5 per cent of the normals as positive (false positives). If, instead, we required only 1 per cent of the cells to exceed these criteria, we would miss only 6 per cent of the cancer patients, but 20 per cent of the normals would then be classed as positive. This reciprocal relationship between false positives and false negatives can be seen more clearly in Figure 6.13, which has been derived from the two

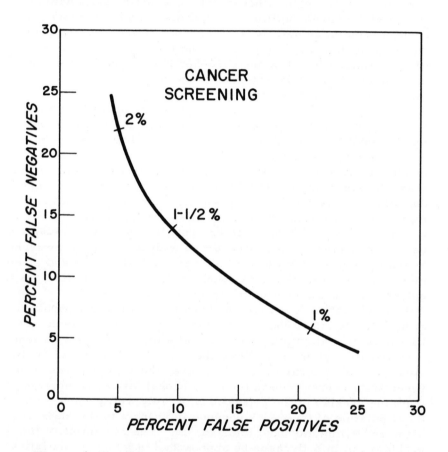

Figure 6.13. Screening curve for data from Figure 6.12.

curves in Figure 6.12 by taking a number of intermediate values of the required percentage of suspicious cells (i.e., those with $d \geq 10\mu$ and $\epsilon > 0.5$). Three different values of the percentage of suspicious cells are marked on the curve. Depending on what value we choose for this percentage, we can operate the screening program at any point on this curve and have the indicated percentages of false negatives and false positives.

Using the basic method outlined above, a whole series of screening curves like the one in Figure 6.13 were constructed, each with a different criterion for suspicious cells. Obviously, if any curve were to lie wholly below any other one, its criterion would yield superior screening results (i. e. , fewer false negatives and false positives). Within limits, the screening curves for a number of different criteria were very much alike, provided that the cells were collected by the methods then prevalent, vaginal aspiration and cervical swab. Thus, this particular diagnostic test, which is based only on counting cells with certain predetermined qualities, will always yield some false positives and false negatives. The point of demarcation between those cases diagnosed as positive and those diagnosed as negative can be arbitrarily set by the screener by requiring a certain percentage of the cells observed to exceed the established criterion for nuclear size and density.

This basic paradigm will be recognized by operations analysts as a problem in statistical decision theory. An optimum position for the point separating the negative and positive cases can be determined by a study of the costs involved for the different combinations of false positives and false negatives which occur along the screening curve (Figure 6. 13). The physician-screener does this unconsciously by expressing a bias for or against treatment. Some physicians, loath to miss a single cancer case, would want this point set at 1 per cent, or even fewer, suspicious cells, while others, more concerned with the workload presented by the false positives which would have to be biopsied and given more thorough examinations, would not consider a smear positive unless it had 2 per cent or more suspicious cells.

This example of a screening operation applied to a population of individuals is, of course, not the same as the problem faced by a physician attempting to arrive at a diagnosis for a patient with specific symptoms. Nevertheless, the elements of the two situations are the same. In each case, there is an element of uncertainty expressible in terms of probabilities and derived from the overlap of the populations of truly well persons with the population of truly sick persons in respect to the medical signs and symptoms used in diagnosis. The resolution of the problem can in both cases be approached in terms of statistical decision theory by determining the costs to the system of false positives and false negatives and arriving at a value of the diagnostic measure which minimizes the total cost to the system.

It might be argued that while the problem of cytological screening for cancer could be reduced to simple quantitative terms, other aspects of medical diagnosis would not lend themselves to such treatment. However, it should be pointed out that before this study was undertaken, cytological diagnosis was considered to be something of an art, and no exact measurements of cell properties were ever employed. The average

screener was a highly skilled technician who had learned to
recognize the "normal" cell and the "suspicious" cell, and if
enough suspicious cells were found on a smear, it was diagnosed as positive. Diagnostic procedures generally rely heavily
on qualitative descriptions of the sort used in cytology, and considerable effort would be needed to place some of them on a
more secure quantitative footing. As an example of a diagnostic
procedure where no previously established quantitative criteria
were employed, we will discuss briefly the results of some
studies on the reliability of chest X-rays in screening a population for tuberculosis.

Roentgenographic Screening for Tuberculosis. The examination of chest X-ray films by a roentgenologist is much like the
study of cells on a microscope slide by a cytologist. The reader
of the X-ray film, examining shadows on the chest plates, uses
certain qualitative criteria based on past experience to classify
patients as either positive or negative for active tuberculosis.
Presumably, a quantitative study of size and density of spots in
the lung shadows could be carried out on patients known to be
either positive or negative for the disease, and sets of screening
curves based on such measurements could be established, exactly
as they were in the cancer problem. However, an ingenious set
of experiments[15],[16] enables us to estimate the false positive and
false negative values in X-ray screening for tuberculosis by
comparing the independent results of several successive screenings. In one study[16] each film in a 70-mm. photofluorogram
survey of a large population was given ten independent interpretations by eight different readers (two readers made two independent interpretations each). If a film was judged negative on
all ten interpretations, it was regarded as "truly negative." If
it was called positive on one or more interpretations, a 14" x 17"
chest plate was taken on the individual and interpreted independently six times. If one or more of these interpretations was
positive, a conference of seven radiologists and chest specialists
examined the plate. If, in the unanimous opinion of this group,
there was evidence of inflammatory disease requiring clinical
follow-up, the case was considered "truly positive." A small
number of "questionable" cases were found in which it was not
possible to arrive at a unanimous opinion. These were eliminated from the study.

It was possible, by defining the "truly negative" and "truly
positive" cases in the manner outlined above, to score the performance of each roentgenologist on his first reading of each
film. The average percentage of the "truly positives" missed
on the first reading by the roentgenologists tested in this study
was 32.2 per cent. At the same time, these readers called
1.7 per cent of the "truly negatives" positive. Since the incidence

of "truly positives" in this particular population was also 1.7
per cent, the false positives picked up by the average reader
would exactly double the caseload for the more rigorous follow-
up examination necessitated by the positive reading.

In this same study[16] an attempt was made to assess the value
of dual reading (i.e., independent judgment of two different
readers to select the positive cases).   There are two ways in
which these judgments can be combined: One can either label
positive only those cases in which both readers agree, or one
can call any case positive for which at least one such opinion
was obtained.   The first method increases the false negatives
but decreases the false positives over those obtained in a single
reading, while the second method decreases the false negatives
but increases the false positives.   The two points obtained in
this manner have been plotted in Figure 6.14 along with the
point obtained for a single reading.   Also shown on this curve
are two further points obtained independently by Garland,[9] who
attempted to assess the effect of the reader's attitude by asking
roentgenologists to read a group of films twice, first with an
optimistic interpretation and then with a much more pessimistic
attitude.   The significant fact in these studies is that all five
points appear to lie on the same curve.   Further evidence of
the existence of such a curve has been obtained recently by
Lusted,[13] who has compiled the results from several other
studies, all of which yield false negative and false positive
values for the reading of chest films that fall on the curve
drawn in Figure 6.14.

The fact that false negatives and false positives again exhibit
the reciprocal relationship which has already been demonstrated
in the cancer-screening problem indicates that the same underlying process is at work here.   There must again be an overlap
between the diseased population and the healthy population with
regard to the amount of the characteristic used to distinguish
the two populations.   In this case, however, we have not yet
established a well-defined quantitative criterion, and at best
we can only describe it as some sort of "built-in" standard
maintained by the individual roentgenographic readers on the
basis of their experience and training.   The results, however,
are exactly the same.   If the X-ray reader looks for smaller
and smaller amounts of the sign used to diagnose the disease,
he will miss fewer true positives but at the same time create
more false positives.   Some further clues as to the nature of
the roentgenographic reading process may be found in the extensive data collected by Yerushalmy.

In the study of dual readings,[16] it was found that two independent readings of the same plates increased the number of the
positive readings among both the true positives and true negatives.

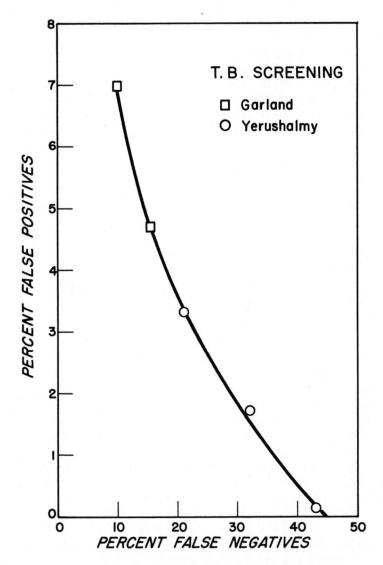

Figure 6.14. Percentages of false positives and false
            negatives obtained in readings of photo-
            fluorograms. Data from Garland[9] and
            Yerushalmy.[16]

Furthermore, the amount of this increase was almost as great
if the same reader made the second set of observations as if
they were carried out by an independent reader. This suggests
that a probabilistic process is involved. In fact, a simple
mathematical model can be constructed by assigning to each
plate a constant probability of being chosen as a positive. The

population of X-ray plates can then be represented by a probability distribution curve, with separate curves for the truly
negative and the truly positive populations. If such curves were
available, it would be possible to determine the number of positives picked up on any number of successive screenings. Crude
probability distribution curves of this sort were constructed
from some more recent data of Yerushalmy[17] in which about
15,000 photofluorograms were each given eight independent
readings. The number of positive readings was obtained for
each plate, so that probabilities of being chosen positive could
be determined for each plate (in units of 0.125) and distribution
curves could be constructed out of the eight points obtained in
this manner. From these two curves, an estimate could be
obtained of the percentage of false positives and false negatives
which would be obtained with one, two, three, etc., screenings.
The curve of false positives versus false negatives again resem-
bles the curve in Figure 6.14. In fact, eight successive screenings would have produced a point almost identical to the one
obtained by Garland when he asked his screeners to be as pessimistic as possible in reading the films. This suggests the
interesting hypothesis that the screeners in Garland's experiment who took the most pessimistic view of the plates were
really looking longer, probably about eight times as long as the
average screener used by Yerushalmy. This is exactly what
one would expect from the theory of search, since the probability
of an observer's detecting a suspicious spot would increase with
the number of glances made at the plate.[11] If the probability of
detection at a single glance is very small, this probability is
approximately linear with time of scanning. If this theory is
correct, then, as long as the observers have the same altert-
ness and competence, doubling the search time of a single
observer is the equivalent of two independent readings.

It appears, therefore, that both the cytological screening
procedure and the chest X-ray scanning procedure can be described as a search problem. The careful screener who spends
a lot of time on each specimen in order not to miss any diseased
cases will detect more of the diseased persons in the population
than one who is willing to accept a higher percentage of suspicious cells in cytological smears or to take a shorter look at
the X-ray plates. However, because of the overlap of the
clinically well and the definitely diseased population in the
amount of the diagnostic sign used to detect the disease, the
more fastidious screener will also pick out more false positives.
Once a screening curve has been established for any diagnosable
disease, the bias of the diagnostician can be determined by observing the percentage of false negatives and false positives
obtained in his samples. In the two examples discussed in this

Chapter, the false positive percentage can be determined routinely, since the patients diagnosed by the screening test are generally given very thorough follow-up tests. Most diagnostic tests have not yet been studied as methodically as the two cited above, and data needed to establish screening curves are not available on the majority of disease states. However, there is no reason why a program of research to establish quantitative criteria of the reliability of medical diagnosis could not be undertaken on all widely prevalent disease complexes.

A Program for Research. It was suggested earlier in this Section that progress in research on medical diagnosis is dependent on the joint efforts of operations research workers and medical scientists. The former are needed for their ability to apply quantitative methods to the decision process, and the latter are needed to provide the basic medical framework in which to apply the mathematical decision models. The approach will have to be largely experimental, much as outlined in the two examples presented in this Section. Only by running such experiments will it be possible to determine how effective each test or diagnostic sign is in separating the healthy from the diseased population. This work can lead in two directions. On the one hand, it can be used to search for better diagnostic tests which will reduce the overlap between the diseased and healthy populations. This is the direction for the medical scientists to work toward. On the other hand, if further research shows that a significant overlap between the diseased and healthy populations continues to be present in the most common disease complexes regardless of the diagnostic tests used, then a careful definition of the costs entailed by misdiagnosis will be required. These can be used by the operational analyst as a basis for formulating decision rules which will minimize the total system costs.

Finally, research on diagnosis should eventually lead to a better definition of illness. Is illness a sharply defined state or a continuum ranging from perfect health to disability? Is everybody ill to some degree, and is the difficulty of finding suitable diagnostic criteria therefore due to the necessity of making an arbitrary division in this continuum? Certainly, the answers to these questions will be functions of the disease under consideration. Certain degenerative diseases probably occur to some extent in everybody, but acute illnesses of various sorts can easily be recognized in the individuals affected. By eliminating the easily diagnosed disease states, attention can be focused on those borderline areas which affect large segments of the population. Research on diagnosis will inevitably contribute to the advance of medical science as a whole.

References

Hospital Operations:
1. Bailey, N. T. J. , "Statistics in Hospital Planning and Design, "
   Journal of the Royal Statistical Society, Applied Statistics,
   5, No. 3, 146-157 (1956).

2. Balintfy, J. L. , "A Stochastic Model for the Analysis and
   Prediction of Admissions and Discharges in Hospitals, "
   in Management Sciences: Models and Techniques, Vol. 2,
   288-299, Pergamon Press, Paris, 1960.

3. Barr, A. , "Measuring Nursing Care -- Operational Research
   in Nursing, " in Problems and Progress in Medical Care,
   77-90, Oxford University Press, 1964.

4. Conner, R. J. , A Hospital Inpatient Classification System,
   Ph. D. Thesis, The Johns Hopkins University, 1960.

5. Fetter, R. B. , and J. D. Thompson, "The Simulation of
   Hospital Systems, " Operations Research, 13, 689-711
   (1965).

6. Flagle, C. D. , "The Problem of Organization for Hospital
   Inpatient Care, " in Management Sciences: Models and
   Techniques, Vol. 2, 275-287, Pergamon Press, Paris,
   1960.

7. Flagle, C. D. , "Operations Research in the Health Services, "
   Operations Research, 10, 591-603 (1962).

8. Young, J. P. , A Queuing Theory Approach to the Control of
   Hospital Inpatient Census, Ph. D. Thesis, The Johns
   Hopkins University, 1962.

Medical Diagnosis:
9. Garland, L. H. , "Scientific Evaluation of Diagnostic Procedure, " Radiology, 52, 309-328 (1949).

10. Horvath, W. J. , W. E. Tolles, and R. C. Bostrom, "Quan-
    titative Measurements of Cell Properties on Papanicolaou
    Smears as Criteria for Screening, " in Transactions of the
    First International Cancer Cytology Congress, 371-397,
    American Cancer Society, Chicago, 1956.

11. Koopman, B. O. , "The Theory of Search. Part II: Target
    Detection, " Operations Research, 4, 503-531 (1956).

12. Ledley, R. S. , and L. B. Lusted, "The Reasoning Founda-
    tions of Medical Diagnosis, " Science, 130, 9-21 (1959).

13. Lusted, L. B. , "Logical Analysis in Roentgen Diagnosis, "
    Radiology, 74, 178-193 (1960).

14. Tolles, W. E., W. J. Horvath, and R. C. Bostrom, "A
    Study of the Quantitative Characteristics of Exfoliated
    Cells from the Female Genital Tract. II: Suitability of
    Quantitative Measurements for Automatic Prescreening,"
    Cancer, 14, 455-468 (1961).

15. Yerushalmy, J., "Statistical Problems in Assessing Methods
    of Medical Diagnosis, with Special Reference to X-ray
    Techniques," Pub. Health Repts., 62, 1432-1449 (1947).

16. Yerushalmy, J., J. T. Harkness, J. H. Cope, and B. R.
    Kennedy, "The Role of Dual Reading in Mass Radiography,"
    Amer. Rev. Tuberculosis, 61, 443-464 (1950).

17. Yerushalmy, J., "The Importance of Observer Error in the
    Interpretation of Photofluorograms and the Value of Mul-
    tiple Readings," in Proceedings of the International
    Congress of Medical Radiography, 219-236, Congress of
    Medical Radiography, Paris, 1956.

Chapter 7

A SYSTEMS APPROACH TO THE STUDY OF
CRIME AND CRIMINAL JUSTICE

Alfred Blumstein
and
Richard C. Larson

7.1 Introduction

This Chapter reports on some attempts to apply systems
analysis to the examination of the criminal justice system --
the system of police, courts, and corrections directed at controlling crime. It is based on work undertaken at the Institute
for Defense Analyses by the Science and Technology Task Force
of the President's Commission on Law Enforcement and Administration of Justice. [5,10]

The Chapter begins with a generalized description of the systems analysis process. It then illustrates how this approach
might be applied to the overall criminal justice system and, in
more detail at a lower level, proceeds to an examination of the
police patrol apprehension system.

The phrase, "system analysis," which has been popularized
during the past five years by technologists and administrators
alike, refers to little more than a systemized logical method of
defining, structuring, and analyzing complex operating systems
in quantitative terms. Much attention in recent months has
focused on applications of the "systems" approach to large-
scale social problems such as public health, housing, education,
welfare, etc. Four recent California studies[1,3,4,9] provide an
example of the method as applied in the public domain. We will
discuss here its application to the problems of the criminal
justice system.

The criminal justice system is an enormous complex of operations. Subjecting such a system to scientific investigation normally involves making changes in its operations in order to
observe the effects directly. Whenever practical, this kind of
controlled experimentation is clearly the best kind. But experimentation inside a system is often impractical and even undesirable, not only because the costs could be prohibitive, but because
normal operations are frequently too critical to be disrupted.
Instead, the scientist may be able to formulate a mathematical

description or "model" of the system in order to illuminate the
relationships among its parts. Systems analysis involves construction and manipulation of such mathematical models in order
to find out how better to organize and operate the real-life systems they represent. It is desirable to conduct such analyses
of the criminal justice system for several reasons:

1. They develop an explicit description of the criminal justice
    system and its operating modes so that the system's under-
    lying assumptions are revealed.
2. They provide a vehicle for simulated experimentation in
    those instances in which "live" experimentation is unfeasi-
    ble.
3. They identify the data that must be obtained if essential
    calculations are to be made of the consequences of pro-
    posed changes.

These advantages must be considered in light of a sober
appreciation of what cannot be done by constructing and using
models. The cause-and-effect relationships in the real world
of criminal justice are so complex and so intricately interwoven
that any mathematical description of them is bound to be a gross
simplification. At the present time, even the most basic relationships are poorly understood, and the available data contribute little to further understanding. Moreover, the causal
relationships themselves are constantly changing and will
change further as increased understanding changes people's
behavior. Clearly, a system of this magnitude and complexity
cannot be studied in detail even descriptively, much less analytically, in a few months by a few people. However, sufficient
benefits have accrued from similar analyses conducted on
equally complex systems, such as air traffic systems and
national economies, to warrant probes in this direction. The
State of California has already supported a pioneering study of
this sort at the Space-General Corporation.[9] The task force
further developed these approaches in order to lay a foundation
on which additional analytical development could be based and
also to identify the primary data needs.

Among the capabilities provided by models is the ability to
conduct cost-effectiveness analyses. These analyses, applied
with particular success in the Department of Defense, provide
a means for determining which of several alternative courses
of action will provide maximum effectiveness for a given cost,
or minimum cost for a given effectiveness. There are many
different measures of both cost and effectiveness applicable to
crime control programs. Numerical costs include direct dollar
costs of operating the criminal justice system, as well as indirect costs such as lost income of offenders who are denied

good jobs. Numerical measures of effectiveness include reductions in the rates of the various crimes. Nonquantitative considerations such as justice, individual liberty, rights of privacy, and freedom from fear of victimization are of vital concern, but are beyond the realm of numerical treatment. The techniques of analysis can be brought to bear only on those parts of crime and criminal justice that are amenable to quantification, and these measurable values must always be considered in relation to what are frequently more important, often unquantifiable, values in making any decisions about modification of police, court, or corrections operations. The cost-effectiveness approach does not force a quantification of unmeasurable human values. Rather, it sets out those implications that are quantifiable, and thereby permits a sharper focus on the critical value questions of social policy by the legislator and the administrator.

7.2   The Systems Analysis Process

Whatever the domain of the study, the first endeavor in any system analysis must be to discover the scope of the system currently being investigated. For instance, in the study of a social system, the agencies to be included in the study must be delineated as well as the interfaces each may have with other "outside agencies." This procedure places the necessary delimiters on the extent of the forthcoming analysis and allows concentrated examination of the defined system.

Once the scope of the system is defined, then the objective of the system and the functions which are performed within it are specified. In the case of social systems, agencies which jointly perform particular functions are grouped together to form "subsystems." For instance, one could define the "corrections subsystem" of the administration of justice system as being composed of all prisons, work-camps, parole boards, and probation officers. Of course, within each subsystem there are smaller units (sub-subsystems), and this partitioning process can continue until the necessary detail of structure is attained. From these initial definitions, a hierarchical structure evolves which provides a preliminary framework upon which to base further analyses.

After the initial system structuring, the question relating to system objectives naturally arises: "Is there a convenient way in which to quantify and express in terms of common units the objectives of the system?" Or, in terms more familiar to the system analyst, "What are the appropriate measures of system effectiveness?" The answer to this question becomes particularly difficult when dealing with ill-defined terms such as "justice," "freedom," and "public safety." Those objectives which cannot be quantified are, of necessity, removed from the analysis with full awareness that subsequent numerical results must be reviewed, taking into consideration the missing factors.

Once we have defined the system objectives, we would like to determine the feasible region within which decisions can be made -- that is, identify the variables under the control of a particular decision maker. Then, the constraints on his decisions must be identified. For instance, the existing criminal law imposes operational constraints on all agencies within the administration of justice system. To a judge, sentencing policies are controllable within the constraints of statutory minimum and maximum sentences.

The discussion to this point has focused simply on defining the system problem. Now the analysis phase commences. Figure 7.1 is a block diagram depicting the iterative system analysis

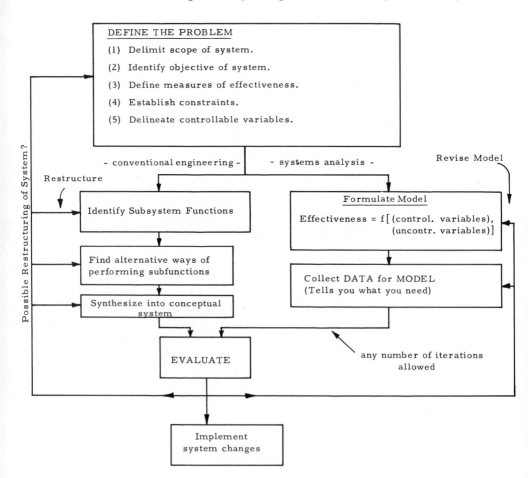

Figure 7.1. The systems analysis and engineering process.

process. The left-hand side shows the conventional engineering process of breaking a task into its parts and finding alternative ways of performing each part.

The right-hand side shows the contribution of systems analysis. Inherent in systems analysis is the formulation of a "model," a mathematical description of the relationship between the measures of effectiveness and the controllable and uncontrollable variables. This model permits a quantitative comparison of alternative system designs represented by different values of the controllable variables in terms of the defined measures of effectiveness. The model identifies the relevant data to be collected and inserted as parameter values for computation of the results.

The process leading to evaluation of alternatives is iterative. Depending on the adequacy of the results, we can reformulate the model, collect new data, restructure part of the system, or redefine the entire problem. Hopefully, as the model becomes more refined and system operating characteristics become more clear, the process converges, at which point a satisfactory basis for system selection is reached.

7.3 System Analysis of Overall Criminal Justice System

Let us now turn to applying this general concept to examining the criminal justice system, composed of three major subsystems: police, courts, and corrections. The general structure of the overall system is shown in Figure 7.2.

With sufficient effort, an adequately complete and detailed model could be developed from the rudimentary, generalized model shown in Figure 7.2. It would permit examination of such questions as:

1. The effects upon court and correctional caseloads and operating costs of a 10 per cent increase in police clearance rates.
2. The effects upon court and correctional costs and workloads of providing counsel to all those arrested.
3. The effects upon costs and arrest rates in a particular State of instituting a given community-treatment program for certain sentenced offenders.
4. The projected workloads and operating costs of police, courts, and corrections for the next five years.
5. The effects upon recidivism and associated costs of statistical techniques that permit sentencing judges to prescribe optimum treatment programs.

However, such analyses require a completeness and detail of description that will take many years of research to develop and will always have elements of uncertainty.

In formulating the model the criminal justice system can be

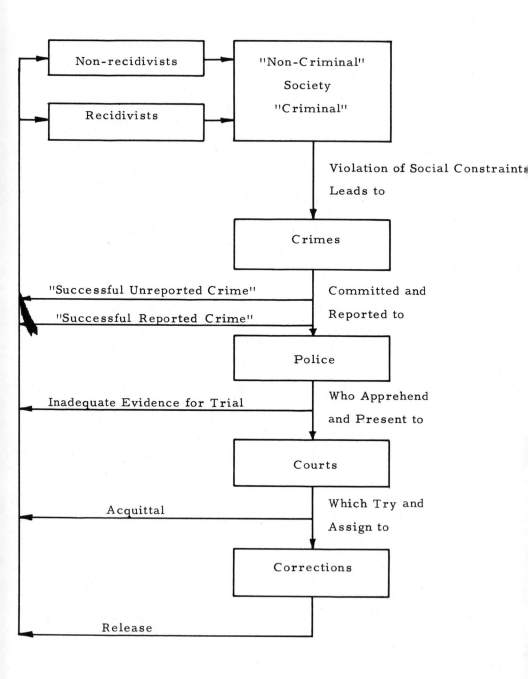

Figure 7.2. Overall criminal justice system.

described as follows: From the general population, which is described by a set of demographic variables, are generated a number of crimes, a subset of which leads to the arrest of people who have not been arrested before. From the subpopulation of former criminals are also generated a number of crimes, a subset of which leads to the rest of those who have been arrested before (recidivists). Following police arrest of both of these types of individuals, as a result of the police system, the arrested persons will either be formally charged with a crime and subsequently introduced to the court system at the magistrate stage or be released from the system with the charges dropped. In the former case, the courts system will eventually find the accused either "guilty" of the original crime or perhaps of some lesser offense, whereupon he is placed into the corrections system; or he is found "not guilty" or is dropped from further proceedings for some other reason. If he is found "guilty," the corrections system can place him in one or more of several states, including incarceration, probation, work-release, and eventually parole and/or release. After the termination of the correctional program, the former convict is reintroduced into society as a member of the subpopulation of former convicts. The flows through the system for the FBI's "index crimes" of murder, forcible rape, aggravated assault, robbery, burglary, larceny of $50 and over, and auto theft are shown in Figure 7.3.[13]

With each of the possible criminal justice system drop-out points is associated a set of probabilities of recidivism, that is, "recommission of crime." Although these probabilities are functionally related to many historical variables, such as number and type of previously committed crimes and age at first arrest, they are controllable, to some extent, by administrative decisions and resulting programs. That is, the probability of recidivism will, to a large extent, depend on how the person is treated within the criminal justice system, and, in particular, at what stage he is dropped out.

In addition, system flows should be partitioned by crime type. That is, since the characteristics of individuals being processed by the criminal justice system depend so heavily on the type of crime with which they are associated, it is necessary to indicate specifically the various crime types in the system. We do this by specifying the number of individuals at any particular point, not by a single number but by an array of numbers (a vector) ordered by crime type. We use the seven index crimes for which extensive data is tabulated yearly by the FBI and other agencies. Thus, each link and each branching point depicted in Figure 7.2 can actually be considered to be a set of seven links or branch points, respectively. Since the flows are partitioned

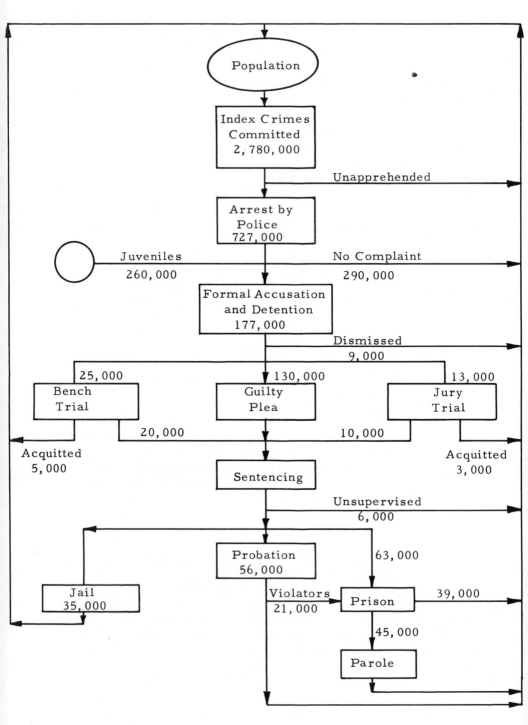

Figure 7.3. Estimated system flow rates for the index crimes.

by crime type, it was necessary to indicate the way in which
recidivists would return to crime. That is, simply knowing
that a person would become arrested again was not sufficient;
we also had to know which crime he would be arrested for,
given the crime for which he was last arrested. We found
limited data[8,12] from which we could specify this relationship
if we defined the following probability:

$P_{ij|R}$ ≡ probability that a person last arrested
for crime type i will next be arrested
for type j, given that he will be arrested
again (i. e. , that recidivism and arrest
occurs) ($1 \leq i, j \leq 7$)

This probability was called a "recidivism transition probability, "
indicating the relative chance of switching to crime type j,
given that the last arrest was for crime type i and that rearrest
occurs. The array of these probabilities was called the "recidivism transition probability matrix. " The matrix used in some
of the studies is shown in Table 7.1. Note that for the so-called
property crimes,* the "on-diagonal" terms are generally higher
than the other terms in the same row, indicating that a recidivist
will more often return to the same crime.** Preliminary analysis indicated that those who do recidivate tend to "escalate" in
seriousness of crime. For instance, a typical criminal career
is started in auto theft (perhaps a joy ride) and could proceed to
burglary, then to robbery, and perhaps to crimes of violence.
     Our model still lacks a description of time delays between
arrests. For instance, it would seem to be desirable to increase the mean time between crimes (and arrests) of those
who will resort to crime again, in order to decrease the overall
number of crimes to be committed during their careers. Fortunately, limited data indicating distributions of times until
recidivism was available for several jurisdictions. Although
the exact numbers are not important, it is relevant to mention
that, of those who do recidivate and are apprehended, approximately 99 per cent do so within five years after release and over
60 per cent within two years after release.[2,6,7] Unfortunately,
these data were not partitioned by crime type, so that all crime
types had to be treated equally with respect to expected time
until recidivism.
     Time delays were introduced by keeping track of the age of
persons in the flow. That is, at any point in the system, the

---

* Robbery, burglary, larceny, and auto theft are the property
   crimes.
** Also, the unconditional probability of re-arrest is higher for
   the property crimes.

Table 7.1. Recidivism Transition Probability Matrix

P_R Last Crime for Which Arrested \ Future Crimes for Which Arrest Will Occur	1	2	3	4	5	6	7
1	0.025	0.025	0.4	0.15	0.2	0.1	0.1
2	0.02	0.15	0.26	0.11	0.2	0.14	0.12
3	0.025	0.04	0.3	0.15	0.085	0.2	0.2
4	0.015	0.015	0.06	0.35	0.35	0.11	0.1
5	0.01	0.02	0.06	0.14	0.46	0.28	0.03
6	0.01	0.02	0.03	0.14	0.4	0.27	0.13
7	0.01	0.027	0.028	0.045	0.39	0.22	0.28

Crime Code

i, j	Crime
1	Criminal homicide
2	Forcible rape
3	Aggravated assault
4	Robbery
5	Burglary
6	Larceny over $50
7	Auto theft

flow is specified not only by numbers of people by crime type, but also by age of offenders, year by year. Also, recidivism probabilities were known to be functionally related to age in a negative linear manner, so that increasing the age of a person in the system decreased his probability of recidivism. The time delays then became simply "age-increasers;" a 21-year-old parolee who is arrested after three years for another index crime is "delayed" three years and emerges as a 24-year-old. This aging facility, accompanied by the age-dependent recidivism probabilities, allows us to trace an individual's criminal career from age at first arrest through to last dismissal from the criminal justice system. We can determine the average number of arrests of individuals in their lifetimes, the types of arrests, and the mean length of the criminal career, all as a function of age at first arrest. Also, we can determine

effects on the overall crime rate caused by changing one or
more of the recidivism probabilities.

Before discussing these capabilities further, let us discuss
two additional features of this model. First, each of the three
major component systems (police, courts, corrections) was
considerably "de-aggregated" so that all important decision
points and related divergences in the flow of individuals through
the system could be seen. Then, costs were assigned to each
substage in the de-aggregated model. Thus, as individuals
proceed through the systems, the costs they incur at each stage
can be added, so that an aggregated cost can be associated with
an individual at any point in the system. The problem of defining
the appropriate costs was considerable. Direct criminal justice
system operating costs lent themselves most readily to definition,
measurement, and insertion into the model. However, this cannot account for the less clearly defined "social costs" related
to the crime, the victim, and the criminal. These social costs
included the disutility of the crime to society and to the victim
in particular, the lost income of the accused while in detention,
the welfare payments to families of detained indigents, and the
expected discounted decrease in lifetime income as a result of
contact with the criminal justice system.

Increasing the detail of the model by de-aggregation and adding
system operating costs to each stage, we can now compute another relevant quantity as a function of age and crime at first
arrest -- a quantity called the "criminal career cost." That is
the expected criminal justice system operating cost which can
be attributed to an individual over his criminal lifetime.

The entire model was programmed on a digital computer and
the costs per crime, the costs per arrest, and calculated criminal career costs of those first arrested at age 16 are depicted
in Table 7.2. As noted in the Table, only a fraction of police
patrol and detective costs is allotted to index-crime arrestees
(felons). Note that the criminal career cost of a 16-year-old
assaulter, for instance, is less than that of a burglar. This by
no means indicates that it is "cost-effective" to persuade would-
be burglars to assault instead; it only indicates the magnitudes
of the quantifiable component of the cost -- the system operating
cost. Recall that the more relevant "social costs" are omitted
from the model, but must be included by system administrators
in weighing any decision. The point here can be applied, in
some degree, to system analyses of any social system. The
analyst can indicate the relationship of quantifiable variables
and system policies, but the fact that numbers are a result of
this phase of the decision-making process, while no numbers
accompany the other phases, does not mean that the decisions
should be based solely upon the "hard" results.

Table 7.2. Total 1965 U. S. Criminal Justice System Costs for Index Crimes[*]

Crime type	Total system costs (millions of dollars)	Number of crimes	System costs per crime (dollars)	Number of arrests	System costs per arrest (dollars)	Career costs[**] (dollars)
Willful homicide	48	9,850	4,900	9,400	5,100	12,600
Forcible rape	29	22,470	1,300	14,300	2,000	9,600
Robbery	140	118,920	1,200	54,300	2,600	13,500
Aggravated assault	190	206,700	920	108,000	1,800	9,400
Burglary	820	1,173,200	700	266,000	3,100	14,000
Larceny of $50 and over	500	762,400	660	144,000	3,500	11,900
Auto theft	370	486,600	760	131,000	2,800	11,000
All Index crimes	2,097	2,780,140	750	727,000	2,900	12,200[***]

[*] 100 per cent of detective force costs and 25 per cent of patrol force costs and court and corrections costs were allocated to index crimes.

[**] Based on index crimes with the first index-crime arrest occurring at age 16 for the indicated crime.

[***] Based on distribution of first arrests matched to distribution of arrests of individuals under 18 given in the 1965 Uniform Crime Reports.

Police Apprehension System Analysis. One can apply this same approach to examining a subsystem of the criminal justice system. In particular, a major effort was directed at analysis of police field operations, focusing especially on the apprehension process.

We define the police apprehension system as being composed of that sequence of logical steps, functions, and activities which are enacted between the start of a crime and final police apprehension of the perpetrator of the crime. Among these steps, functions, and activities are included detection of the crime, communication of that fact to the police, police response, search of the crime scene, and investigative work (providing apprehension is not immediate).

In the analysis, emphasis was placed upon rapid or "hot" apprehension at the crime scene, which is a major way in which suspects are arrested.

Although arrest statistics are widely available, there is very little information relating apprehensions to various operational factors or policies.

We focused on two variables of primary interest, one for each way the apprehension process can be initiated. For a crime detected in progress by a patrolman, the basic variable was the probability of detection. For a crime detected other than by the police (e.g., witness detection), the police system response time was the primary focus. Thus, the effectiveness of the apprehension system depends on patrol detection and on the sequence of delays which occur in responding to calls for help. Some of the policies affecting both of these are adjustable by administrative decisions (e.g., intensity of patrol and density of cars on the street) and have associated system costs.

The modeling of the preventive patrol function would cause police administrators to be aware of the interrelationships among the fractions of time on patrol, speed of the patrolling unit, crime intensity, and crime detectability. Likewise, determination of the magnitude and frequency of each of the subsystem delays in terms of descriptive parameters results in the pinpointing of those subsystems contributing the largest fractions of the overall average delay and the ways to reduce this delay.

In general, the occurrence of crimes follows a density function that depends on time and location. However, in the analysis, events were assumed to occur uniformly in time and space. This assumption does not restrict the applicability of the method, because either time or spatial dependence or both can be incorporated simply by constructing a set of uniform models, appropriately interlinking them and restructuring the time and space domain of each.

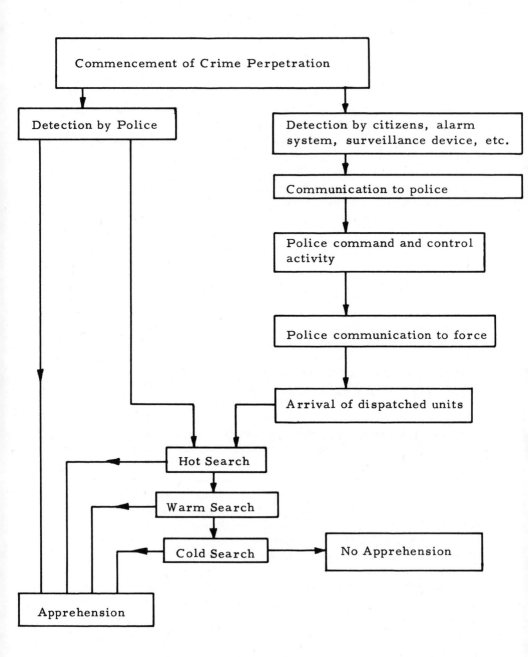

Figure 7.4. The apprehension process.

The steps or functions in the apprehension process are as follows (see figure 7.4):

1. Commencement of crime perpetration.
2. Detection of crime.
3. Communication to police.
4. Police command and control activity.
5. Police communication to force.
6. Arrival of dispatched unit (5).
7. "Hot" search of crime scene.
8. "Warm" search of near-by area.
9. "Cold" investigatory search.

Time delays are associated with each of these steps.

If equations relating each of the subfunction delays and the preventive patrol detection frequencies to relevant cost-dependent system parameters were known, it would be possible to allocate manpower and equipment resources throughout the systems optimally, so that each dollar allocated purchased a maximum amount of decrease in delay time or increase in detections. In order to express returns from various allocation alternatives in terms of a common denominator, dollars, we define two "figures of merit" to be applied to each subfunction:

$NSPD_i \equiv$ average Number of Seconds of delay reduction Per additional Dollar allocated to the ith subsystem

$NAPD_j \equiv$ average Number of additional detections and Apprehensions Per Dollar allocated to the jth subsystem

The numerical values taken on by these variables for each subfunction indicate the marginal returns per dollar of additional resource allocations to that subfunction in terms of common overall system units -- apprehensions, seconds, and dollars.

An outline of the method of police apprehension system analysis is given in Table 7.3. Several sets of subsystem delays and associated allocatable resources are given in Table 7.4.

Patrol Detection Model. We can illustrate the development of one of the very simple models, that is, one of random patrol detection. Specifically, we are interested in characterizing the rate of detections of crimes in progress by patrolling police units. Although we will not specifically address the particular method of patrol manpower allocation, we will assume that a "random patrol" strategy is employed so that the necessary element of surprise is incorporated in the patrol strategy. Then we can assume that the position of the crime or incident is independent of the particular position of the patrol units at any given time.

Table 7.3. Method of Police Apprehension System Analysis

1. Motivation: Higher Apprehension Probability Leads to Deterrence and Crime Prevention.

2. Examining "Hot" Apprehension.

3. Two Variables of Interest:

    Number of Apprehensions Per Year.

    Number of Seconds of Delay Time.

4. Two Figures of Merit for Individual Subsystems:

    Number of Additional Apprehensions Per Dollar Allocated.

    Number of Seconds Saved in Response Time Per Dollar Allocated.

5. Each Subsystem Time is Modelled in Terms of Equations. Figures of Merit Are Then Calculated Using Typical System Parameter Values.

6. Tradeoffs Among Subsystems are Examined.

7. Tentative Conclusions and Recommendations are Presented.

8. Necessary Experiments to Validate the Conclusions and Substantiate the Recommendations are Suggested.

Table 7.4. Apprehension System Delays and Associated Allocatable Resources

Delay	Resource
Time Until Detection	Patrol Units, Sensors, Alarms
Time from Detection Until Obtaining a Police Communications Station	Police Call Boxes, Citizens' Alarm, Telephone Booth, Street Sensors
Telephone Queue Waiting Time	Telephone Clerks
Command and Control Function Delay Time	Equipment, Personnel
Patrol Car Response Time	Patrol Units (as a Function of Speed), Car Location Devices

While active in the field, each patrol unit is characterized by one of two states: State 1) servicing a call or "out of patrol service;" or State 2) performing preventive patrol or "in patrol service." We assume that random detections of crime can occur only in State 2.

Let us assume that the city of interest is characterized by an area A with K patrol units in the field, each unit being responsible for patrolling a district of area $\frac{A}{K}$. We wish to investigate the parameters necessary to describe detection and apprehension probabilities, the interrelationships of these parameters, and the cost of changing the values of various parameters. We define the following:

$\rho \equiv$ probability a patrol unit is patrolling (as opposed to servicing a call)

$S \equiv$ average speed of a patrol unit while performing preventive patrol

$a_j \equiv$ average density of j type crimes per unit time per square mile throughout the city

$T_j \equiv$ average duration of j type crimes

$P_j \equiv$ probability of patrol detection of a j type crime given space-time coincidence

$D_j \equiv$ average number of j type crime detections in a given patrol district per unit time

$\mu \equiv$ average rate of incoming calls for service to patrol units

$\frac{1}{\lambda} \equiv$ average time required for a patrol unit to service one call

$B \equiv$ number of linear street miles per square mile

Assume ST_j (the distance traveled by patrol during commission of the crime) is less than $\frac{BA}{K}$ (the street mileage within the patrol district) by approximately a half order of magnitude or more. Then, given that a j type crime occurs somewhere in the district, and that the crime and patrol positions are independent and uniformly distributed, and that the patrol car is in State 2, the probability of space-time coincidence of crime and patrol is given by

$$\frac{ST_j}{\frac{BA}{K}}$$

Since the patrol unit is performing preventive patrol with a probability ρ,

$$\dfrac{\rho ST_j}{\dfrac{BA}{K}}$$

is the probability of space-time coincidence for a randomly
chosen crime. Given space-time coincidence, the probability
of detection is P_j. During a unit of time the average number of
j type crimes occurring in a patrol district is $a_j \dfrac{A}{K}$. Combining
our results, we obtain

$$D_j = \rho \, \dfrac{ST_j}{\dfrac{BA}{K}} \, P_j \, a_j \dfrac{A}{K} = \rho \, \dfrac{ST_j}{B} \, P_j \, a_j \qquad (7.1)$$

We can easily determine ρ in terms of μ, λ, and K, providing
K is large enough so that there are always patrol units available
to answer calls. We note that

$$\dfrac{K}{\mu} = \text{average time between dispatch orders for one car}$$

Then,

$$\dfrac{\dfrac{1}{\lambda}}{\dfrac{K}{\mu}} = \text{average fraction of time spent servicing calls}$$

$$= \dfrac{\mu}{K\lambda}$$

$$= \text{probability that a random car is \underline{not} available}$$

$$= 1 - \rho$$

Substituting into Equation 7.1 for ρ we have,

$$D_j = (1 - \dfrac{\mu}{K\lambda}) \, \dfrac{ST_j}{B} \, P_j \, a_j \qquad (7.2)$$

If we now define

$$D_{C_j} \equiv \text{average number of j type crime detections}$$
throughout the city per unit time, then we
have finally,

$$D_{C_j} = KD_j = (K - \frac{\mu}{\lambda}) \frac{ST_j}{B} P a_j \qquad (7.3)$$

The factor $(K - \frac{\mu}{\lambda})$ represents the average number of patrol units in State 2 at any time, and might be considered to be "the effective preventive patrol strength."

Using Equation 7.3, we now wish to obtain an estimate of the number of opportunities to detect crimes which patrolmen can expect during any given time interval. For one large U. S. city,[11] the following parameter estimates were obtained:

$K = 270$ patrol units

$A = 460$ square miles

$\mu = 1,700$ calls per day

$\frac{1}{\lambda} = .0208$ days per call

$S = 12$ miles per hour

$B = 14$ linear street miles per square mile

For the crime of burglary, the following two values were also needed:

$a = 0.259$ burglaries per day per square mile

$T = \frac{1}{3}$ hour (assumed)

If we set P to unity in Equation 7.3, we will find the number of times that burglary and patrol obtain space-time coincidence in a day. This number could be interpreted as being the maximum number of patrol opportunities for detecting burglaries in progress. Substituting in Equation 7.3, we find that approximately 17 patrol burglary-in-progress detection opportunities occur each day in this city. This represents approximately 14 per cent of all burglaries committed in one day. In terms of the individual patrol officer who works a 40-hour week, he can expect a maximum of four burglary-in-progress detection opportunities per year.

We need change only two parameters in Equation 7.3 to obtain an estimate of the number of robbery detections per day in our city:

$T = \frac{1}{30}$ hour (assumed)

$a = 0.04$ robberies per day per square mile

Substituting these new values we obtain approximately 0.27 robbery-in-progress detection opportunities per day throughout the city. This represents approximately only two per cent of all robberies committed. The individual patrol officer can expect to detect a robbery-in-progress no more often than once every 14 years.

Although these results are in no way confirmed by required experimentation, they do provide a basis for discussion of the preventive-patrol operating characteristics and its related functions and objectives. The derived formula also indicates, under admittedly simplified assumptions, the relevant system parameters required to describe patrol detection probabilities and the functional role played by each. Thus, the police administrator can immediately say, "There are basically four ways to increase the detection rate described by the analyst's model: 1) Increase K, the number of patrol units; 2) Increase P, the detection probability, given space-time coincidence; 3) Increase S, the average speed of the patrolling vehicle; 4) Reduce the mean service time for each dispatchable call." If costs could be associated with each of these alternatives, then an effective structure for decision-making is formulated.

Other topics of the police apprehension system analysis include the following:

1. Preliminary modeling of certain command and control function features and of the patrol unit field response time.
2. Preliminary study of urban police call-box and citizens' alarms systems.
3. A cost-effectiveness approach to allocating resources efficiently to reduce response time.
4. A set of recommendations ranging from hardware implementation suggestions to recommended overall plans for future study and research.

7.4 Summary

In this Chapter we have discussed the system analysis process as applied to the study of crime and criminal justice. First, the overall administration-of-justice system, composed of police, courts, and corrections was discussed from a modeling viewpoint. Then, the more sharply defined area of police apprehension was outlined and a patrol detection model which describes a portion of the apprehension system was presented.

The study discussed in this Chapter illustrates one method of approach to the analysis of complex social systems. Rather than attempting to describe explicitly individual human behavior, upon which system operations are based, this approach uses macroscopic models and empirically derived data to express the behavior implicitly. This type of analysis provides researchers, decision makers, and other system operatives with another way of studying the relations among actions taken to achieve desired social goals. It provides the capability to test the consequences of alternative actions in the design and operation of social systems and to arrive at a set of decisions which will best achieve the desired objectives.

The same approach is currently being applied in the fields of education, urban planning, and transportation, and in the coming years should provide beneficial insight into operational problems in these areas, as well as in the field of crime and criminal justice.

References

1. California Integrated Transportation Studies, North American Aviation, Inc., Los Angeles, California, 1965.

2. California Prisoners, 1961, 1962, 1963, Administrative Statistics Section, Research Division, Department of Corrections, State of California, Sacramento, California.

3. California Statewide Information System Study, Lockheed Missile and Space Corp., Sunnyvale, California, July, 1965.

4. California Waste Management Study (A Report to the State of California), Department of Public Health, Aerojet-General Corp., El Monte, California, August, 1965.

5. The Challenge of Crime in a Free Society, A Report by the President's Commission on Law Enforcement and Administration of Justice, U. S. Government Printing Office, Washington, D. C., 1967.

6. Crime in California, 1964, Bureau of Criminal Statistics, Division of Criminal Law and Enforcement, Department of Justice, State of California, California Office of State Printing, 1965.

7. Delinquency and Probation in California, 1964, Bureau of Criminal Statistics, Division of Criminal Law and Enforcement, Department of Justice, State of California.

8. Mandel, M. G., et al., "Crime Revisited: A Study of Recidivism of 446 Inmates Released from the Minnesota State Reformatory for Men During July 1, 1955 - June 30, 1956," Minnesota Department of Corrections, 1963.

9. Prevention and Control of Crime and Delinquency in California (Final Report), Space-General Corp. , El Monte, California, 1965.

10. Report of the Science and Technology Task Force of the President's Commission on Law Enforcement and Administration of Justice, U. S. Government Printing Office, Washington, D. C. , 1967.

11. Statistical Digest, 1964, Los Angeles Police Department, Los Angeles, California, 1965.

12. Statistical Tables, Fiscal Year 1965, Federal Bureau of Prisons, U. S. Government Printing Office, Washington, D. C.

13. Uniform Crime Reports for the United States, 1965, Federal Bureau of Investigation, U. S. Department of Justice, U. S. Government Printing Office, Washington, D. C.

Chapter 8

MATHEMATICAL TECHNIQUES:
PROBABILISTIC MODELS

George P. Wadsworth

The concepts and techniques touching on the theory of probability which are of value in understanding certain of these Chapters will be covered here. A short course in probability in a few pages is an almost impossible task, but this material will cover some concepts for those who have not studied probability before, and will also give consideration to the more important techniques in order to develop at least a partial background for the technical understanding of this volume.

One of the concepts involved in the solution of many operations research problems is the use of stochastic mathematical models to simulate the operations under consideration. In the building up of mathematical models of this type, the concept of probability as it is to be defined for the problems considered is basic. From the practical point of view, particularly as it is used in operations research, the probability is defined when and only when the problem is defined. It is most essential that one realizes that this is the case, because often one reads in the literature different analyses of what is purported to be the same problem and different conclusions are often arrived at through analysis. In each case, however, one should observe that the problem is defined in a slightly different manner each time, and therefore the probability itself has a different meaning; this, of course, often accounts for the different conclusions arrived at by the different authors.

It is very clear that when the problem is properly defined, the modus operandi which generates the probability is also uniquely defined. In order to illustrate how very careful one must be to identify completely the method by which the probability is generated, let us consider a simple problem, one in which we take a circle drawn on a piece of paper and pass it around among a large group of people, asking each of them to draw a chord in the circle. We might then ask the question, "What is the probability or the percentage of the chords drawn by the group that might be expected to be longer than the side of an inscribed equilateral triangle?" There are many solutions

181

to this problem, depending upon the assumptions that one makes.

8.1 Alternative Assumptions

For example, represent the random chord as AB (see Figure 8.1a) and construct a tangent to the circle at one end of the chord. If one assumes that this random chord is equally likely to make any angle ϕ with the tangent in the range from 0° to x, it is clear that one third of the chords will lie within the vertex of the equilateral triangle ACD and will therefore have a length greater than that of the side of the triangle. Therefore, since this favorable range producing a chord longer than the side of the triangle is one third of the total range for the angle, the probability might be assumed to be one third.

In a second analysis, the chord chosen at random is now bisected by a radius of the circle (see Figure 8.1b). Let the intersection of the radius with the random chord be X and let the intersection of the radius with the equilateral triangle, placed as in the Figure, be Y. The center of the circle is at 0.

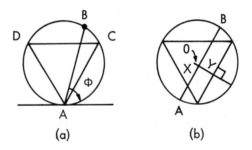

Figure 8.1. Drawing chords in a circle.

It is now clear that if the chord lies between 0 and Y, it will be longer than the side of the equilateral triangle; otherwise, it will be less. The distance from the center to Y is, however, one half the radius, so one would assume that the probability is now one half. Thus, two different answers are obtained because the initial assumptions are incompatible in the two cases. That is, if the values of the angle are what is termed "equally likely," then the values along the diameter are not equally likely and vice versa. In fact, almost any answer to the original question could be obtained by the proper choice of assumptions which define the probability. The difficulty is, of course, that the way in which each person in the original group

decides how to draw a chord is not uniquely defined, and therefore our answer is certainly subjective. It is often this very
difficulty which produces contradictory answers to the same
problems, although the actual mathematical analysis based on
the assumptions is probably correct in each case. <u>The probability is thus defined when the problem is uniquely defined, and,
with the definition of the problem, the method by which the
probability is generated is also specified.</u>

8.2 Lines and Areas

It is clear, for example, what we mean by "picking a point
at random on a line of length L." The line is divided into a
large number of segments which are numbered from 1 to n
(Figure 8.2). It is assumed that the divisions are so small in

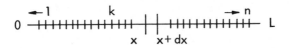

Figure 8.2. Random point on a line.

width and thus so numerous in number that perhaps two pencil
dots inside one division would be indistinguishable to the eye.
Each number from 1 to n, representing the n divisions, is
written on poker chips and these chips placed in a hat. One of
them is drawn at random from the hat, and the number drawn
determines the specific point on the line. It is clear that we
have now defined completely the game that is to be played and
have defined, for example, the probability that the point will
be chosen from the first third of the line; it is obviously a
third, since the percentage of poker chips in the hat representing points in this section of the line is one third of the total.
In fact, the probability that a point chosen at random will fall
between x and x + dx is $\frac{dx}{L}$. It is thus incorrect to talk about
the probability that a specific value or a specific point occurs
on a random draw, since that probability is 0; but rather, by
the probability of the occurrence of a specific value of x, we
mean the probability that it lies in the interval between x and
x + dx.

Let us consider the line AB in Figure 8.3. One section of
the line is <u>a</u> and the other section is <u>b</u>, where a > b. A random
point X is chosen on the interval <u>a</u> and a random point Y chosen
on the interval <u>b</u>. The points X and Y divide the line AB into
three parts, namely, AX, XY, YB. What is the probability
that these three segments form a triangle? Denoting the three

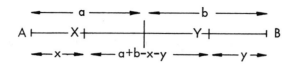

Figure 8.3. Two random points on a line.

sections as x, a + b - x - y, y, as in Figure 8.3, then the
necessary condition that any two of the random lengths has a
sum which is greater than the third one leads to the three
inequalities:

$$x < \frac{a+b}{2}, \quad y < \frac{a+b}{2}, \quad x + y > \frac{a+b}{2}$$

It is clear that if we consider the two-dimensional graph of
the possible region for x and y together with these inequalities
(Figure 8.4), the shaded area represents that portion of the
possible simultaneous values of x and y which satisfy the conditions that the three segments will form a triangle. Since the
probability that x will lie between x and x + dx is $\frac{dx}{L}$ and, simultaneously, the probability that y will lie between y and y + dy is
$\frac{dy}{L}$, then the simultaneous probability (joint probability) that
these two events will occur together is a product of the two
probabilities, or $\frac{dxdy}{ab}$ (since the events are independent),
which represents a small element of area in Figure 8.4. Thus,
the total probability that a triangle will result from our experiment is the summation of the $\frac{dxdy}{ab}$ over the shaded area in
Figure 8.4 divided by the area of the total rectangle (represen-
ting all possible outcomes), which is $\frac{b^2}{2}$ divided by ab, or $\frac{b}{2a}$.
This illustrates the type of problem in which the experiment

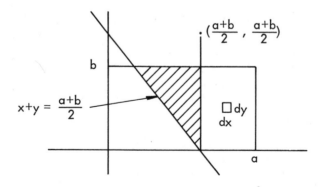

Figure 8.4. Shaded area represents allowed configuration.

being conducted is completely defined and, simultaneously, the probability is completely defined. This analysis would indicate that if we chose these two points X and Y simultaneously N times in a row, we would expect to have a situation in which no triangle could be constructed from the three segments $(1 - \frac{b}{2a})$ times on the average.

8.3 Distribution Functions

Up to this point we have discussed the probability of a specific event occurring, in this particular case, the chance that we can construct a triangle from the three chosen segments. In fact, there are only two possible outcomes to our experiment, namely, either we can form a triangle or we cannot. We might designate these two values as x = 1 and x = 0. More generally, however, we are usually considering an experiment in which a large number of outcomes can occur, either finite or infinite in number. However, in any event, they form an exhaustive set of possibilities, in that the result of the experiment belongs to this finite or infinite set of possibilities. We can then examine a function F(x) which tells us the probability that the random variable x will take on a given value x or less, where x indicates an outcome. This can be done, of course, only under the assumption that there is a one-to-one correspondence between possible events which may occur, and the real-number scale designated as x. F(x) is called the <u>distribution</u> <u>function</u> defined for all x and has the property that $F(-\infty) = 0$ and $F(\infty) = 1$. If there exists a finite probability that the variate x will take on a specific value, then of course the distribution function takes a jump at this particular value; and if we are dealing with a variate which consists entirely of discrete values, then the distribution function consists entirely of jumps, and that portion of the function between these values consists of horizontal lines, as shown in Figure 8.5a. Since F(x) is not defined at one of these jumps, we shall define it such that $F(x) = F(x + 0)$, or the

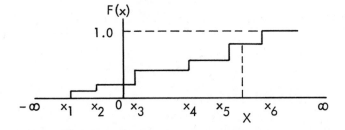

Figure 8.5a. Plot of discrete distribution function.

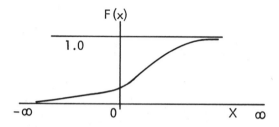

Figure 8. 5b. Plot of continuous distribution function.

value of x is defined as the limit approached from the right. In the particular case where $F(x)$ is continuous (see Figure 8. 5b), or in the case where it is continuous over some region of its definition, it is possible to differentiate this function over that region such that $dF(x) = f(x)dx$. In this instance, $f(x)$ is called the <u>probability density,</u> and thus the probability that the variate will take on a value between x and x + dx is given by $f(x)dx$. In the case that there exists a finite probability at the point x_i, the value will be denoted by $f(x_i)$.

8. 4 Binomial Distribution

Returning again to the triangle problem previously discussed, we have estimated the probability that on a single trial we will be able to form a triangle from the component parts. Obviously, if we conduct this experiment N times, in general there is a very small probability that we would be unable to form this triangle in any one of the N attempts. There is also a small probability, in general, that we would be completely successful by succeeding all N times. Actually, of course, there are N + 1 possible outcomes of the N trials, ranging all the way from these two extremes. Since one of the N + 1 possible outcomes, such as, for example, k successes and N - k failures, must occur, they form an exhaustive set of possibilities and therefore constitute a distribution function $F(x)$ which is similar to that shown in Figure 8. 5a. Each of the jumps on the $F(x)$ axis which occur in the function at the integer values 0 to N + 1, have the value

$$\frac{N!}{x!\,(N-x)!}\left(\frac{b}{2a}\right)^{x}\left(1-\frac{b}{2a}\right)^{N-x} \quad ,$$

which represents the probability of the occurrence of that particular outcome. This probability function is one of the simplest functions we deal with in probability theory and it is

known as the <u>binomial probability distribution</u> because it represents the individual terms of an expansion of $(q + p)^N$, where
p is the probability of success and q is the probability of failure, where $p + q = 1$.

Let us return again to this same problem involving the construction of the triangle. Let the segment of the straight line
represented by <u>a</u> become extremely large compared to the
segment <u>b</u>. Also let the number of trials N increase without
limit in such a way that this increase in N is proportional to
the increase in <u>a</u> as $N = ka$. Thus, the probability of success
on an individual trial $\frac{b}{2a}$ approaches zero at the same time
that the number of trials becomes extremely large, but the
product of the two quantities $(N \cdot \frac{b}{2a})$ remains constant and is
equal to, let us say, λ, where λ is obviously the average number of successful attempts to form a triangle in this experiment.
(The probability of success on an individual trial times the
number of trials is the average number of successes.)

8.5 Poisson Distribution

It is clear that the probability distribution represented by the
"binomial" had two parameters p and N which characterized
the distribution, whereas, if we consider the limiting distribution, we have only one parameter λ. This limiting distribution
has many applications, due to its interesting properties. It is
called the Poisson distribution and has the following formula
for the probability of exactly x successes:

$$p(x) = \frac{e^{-\lambda}\lambda^x}{x!} \qquad x = 0, 1, 2, 3, \ldots, n, \ldots \ .$$

Thus, one might say that the probability of exactly x successes
is given in terms of a single parameter which is the average
number of expected successes, namely, λ. The actual graph
of the distribution function F(x) has therefore an infinite number of jumps which take place at the integer values of x, since
it is only at these integer values that any probability other than
zero exists. The sum of the infinite series of the jump values
when added together must, of course, sum to unity.

Because of the many mathematical models which involve the
Poisson distribution in one way or another, it might be worth
while to examine this mathematical expression a little further.
It is possible to derive the Poisson distribution in a manner
which appeals to one's physical intuition rather than to derive
it as the limit of another mathematical expression.

One might consider, for example, a series of emanations
coming from a particular radioactive source. The average

number of arrivals per unit time has a constant value k, although the number which arrive in any given unit of time is, of course, subject to statistical fluctuation peculiar to the random source. Let us assume that the probability of the occurrence (or arrival at our instrument) of an event in time dt is proportional to the magnitude of dt, where the proportionality factor is k. Thus, k dt is the average number of arrivals in time dt. If at the same time it is assumed that the emanations (events) arrive individually and collectively at random, thus making the probability of two or more events occurring simultaneously in the interval dt an infinitesimal of higher order (i. e., proportional to $(dt)^2$), then it is possible to set up a recursion expression which relates the probabilities involved. If one lets $P(y, T)$ be the probability of exactly y events occurring in time T, then the expression for the probability that there are n emanations arriving in the interval t + dt follows, where we equate the probability that there are n events occurring in the interval t + dt to the probability that there are n in t and none in dt, n - 1 in t and 1 in dt, n - 2 in t and 2 in dt, etc.

$$P(n, t + dt) = P(n, t) P(0, dt) + P(n - 1, t) P(1, dt)$$
$$+ P(n - 2, t) P(2, dt) + \dots .$$

Now, if one substitutes

$$P(1, dt) = k\, dt$$

and

$$P(0, dt) = 1 - P(1, dt) = 1 - k\, dt,$$

the following differential equation results which may be solved recursively for n = 0, 1, ..., if in addition we assume that

$$P(-1, t) = 0$$

and, of course,

$$P(r, dt) = 0 \text{ for } r > 1.$$

$$\frac{dP(n, t)}{dt} + k\, P(n, t) = k\, P(n - 1, t)$$

The solution is the Poisson distribution arrived at before, if one assumes general differentiability conditions for the variable x and also sets $kt = \lambda$.

8.6 Exponential Distribution

If we examine this Poisson distribution from this latter view-point, it is now possible to talk about and to examine the inter-arrival time between events (emanations). It is quite easy to demonstrate that the probability that the interarrival time be-tween any two events will be between t and t + dt is

$$\frac{1}{\theta} e^{-\frac{t}{\theta}} dt,$$

where θ is the average interarrival time of all events. The exponential distribution has a very important property which permits us to set up many mathematical models under the assumption that our events occur individually and collectively at random. If one examines Figure 8.6, which is the graph of

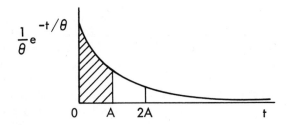

Figure 8.6. Exponential distribution function.

the exponential function (interarrival time), one can see that the probability that an arrival will occur between t = 0 and t = A is represented by the shaded area. One may also com-pute the probability of an arrival occurring between t = A and t = 2A, given the fact that no arrival had occurred up to the time t = A. A similar calculation can be made for the condi-tional probability that an event will occur between 2A and 3A, given that it had not occurred up to the time t = 2A. These three computations are given as a, b, and c as follows:

a) $P(0 - A) = \int_{0}^{A} \frac{1}{\theta} e^{-t/\theta} dt = 1 - e^{-A/\theta}$

b) $P(A - 2A /\text{not } 0 - A) = \dfrac{\int_{A}^{2A} \frac{1}{\theta} e^{-t/\theta} dt}{\int_{A}^{\infty} \frac{1}{\theta} e^{-t/\theta} dt} = 1 - e^{-A/\theta}$

c) $P(2A - 3A/\text{not } 0 - 2A) = \dfrac{\displaystyle\int_{2A}^{3A} \dfrac{1}{\theta} e^{-t/\theta} dt}{\displaystyle\int_{2A}^{\infty} \dfrac{1}{\theta} e^{-t/\theta} dt} = 1 - e^{-A/\theta}$

Since all of these probabilities are identical, the probability
that an event will occur in a time period T is exactly the same,
independent of any past history.   This important property means
that if you enter the system at any random time, the probability
that an emanation will occur in an interval T is exactly the
same as if you had started counting from the moment that a
known event had occurred.   The usefulness of this concept will
be exploited by considering a simple queuing problem later.

8.7 Expected Value

The words "expected value" have been used several times
and perhaps a specific definition is in order now.   Suppose that
a particular experiment gives rise to a series of possible outcomes (either finite or infinite) and that it is known what the
gain or loss is if any one of the particular outcomes occurs.
For example, a man might pay $1.00 for the privilege of tossing
a single die with six sides.   If a 1, 2, or 3 is the result of the
toss, he will be paid $2.00.   If a 4 or 5 occurs he will be paid
$3.00, but if a 6 occurs, he will have to pay $12.00.   The expected value of this game is the probability of each event that
could occur, times the gain or loss if that event does occur.
Thus, the expected value of this game is:

$$\text{Expected value} = \frac{1}{2}(2.00) + \frac{1}{3}(3.00) + \frac{1}{6}(-12.00) = 0$$

Since the value of the game is zero and our man paid $1.00 for
the privilege of tossing the die, the net loss to him per game is
-$1.00.   In general, if we are dealing with a probability density
function such that the probability that x will fall between x and
x + dx is f(x)dx, then the expected value of a continuous function $\phi(x)$ is

$$E(\phi(x)) = \int_{a}^{b} \phi(x)f(x)dx,$$

where the $\phi(x)$ indicates the gain or loss to us for every value
of x where f(x) is defined, and where, of course,

$$\int_a^b f(x)dx = 1.$$

In order to illustrate these ideas in a way which perhaps will make the material in this volume more understandable to those who are not acquainted with these concepts, three simple examples will be considered. The first one deals with maximization of expected value; the second involves distribution functions; and the last considers the solution of a simple waiting line.

Example 8.1. A player is to be rewarded with an amount of money equal to x, where he chooses x according to the following mechanism: He makes a random draw from a population with density

$$f(x) = \begin{cases} 1 & 0 < x < 1 \\ 0 & \text{elsewhere} \end{cases}$$

If he wishes, he may keep this value of x. If not, he may discard it permanently and make another random draw. The procedure may be repeated for a total of three draws. What is the best strategy to follow and thus what is the maximum expected reward?

The strategy obviously involves the value of λ below which value he will discard the drawn value of x and above which he will accept it for each of the three opportunities. Let λ_1 be the dividing value for draw No. 1 and λ_2 that for draw No. 2. The third attempt must be accepted whatever its value. Also let

$$P_1 = \int_{\lambda_1}^1 dx = (1 - \lambda_1)$$

be the probability that our player keeps the first draw and

$$P_2 = \int_{\lambda_2}^1 dx = (1 - \lambda_2)$$

be the probability that he keeps the second draw, given that he rejects the first. Clearly, the expected monetary value of the first draw is $(\frac{1 + \lambda_1}{2})$, of the second draw is $(\frac{1 + \lambda_2}{2})$, and of the third draw is $(\frac{1}{2})$. Thus, the expected value E of the game is

$$E = (1 - \lambda_1)(\frac{1 + \lambda_1}{2}) + \lambda_1(1 - \lambda_2)(\frac{1 + \lambda_2}{2}) + \frac{\lambda_1 \lambda_2}{2}$$

$$= \frac{1}{2}(1 - \lambda_1{}^2) + \frac{\lambda_1}{2}(1 - \lambda_2{}^2) + \frac{\lambda_1 \lambda_2}{2}$$

For a maximum it is necessary that

$$\frac{\partial E}{\partial \lambda_1} = 0 = -\lambda_1 + \frac{1}{2}(1 - \lambda_2{}^2) + \frac{\lambda_2}{2}$$

$$\frac{\partial E}{\partial \lambda_2} = 0 = -\lambda_1 \lambda_2 + \frac{\lambda_1}{2}$$

and thus $\lambda_2 = \frac{1}{2}$ and $\lambda_1 = \frac{5}{8}$, giving a value of $E = .695$, which is a maximum.

Example 8.2. A problem often found in the literature to illustrate the idea of the best distribution of effort deals with a secretary looking for a piece of correspondence which may be in any one of N file folders. The time to search the ith folder is t_i and the probability of finding the letter there is p_i. What is the order in which the folders should be searched in order to minimize the expected search time?

Assuming any searching sequence is adopted, then the probability of finding the correspondence between τ and $\tau + d\tau$ is

$$p(\tau)d\tau = \frac{p_i}{t_i} d\tau,$$

if τ falls in the ith file, or

$$\sum_{i=1}^{i-1} t_i < \tau < \sum_{i=1}^{i} t_i.$$

Thus $p(\tau)$ for any ordering is shown in Figure 8.7a where, of course,

$$\sum_{i=1}^{N} p_i = 1$$

and

$$\sum_{i=1}^{N} t_i = T,$$

the total time to search all folders.

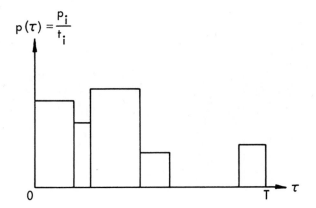

Figure 8. 7a. The quantity $\dfrac{P_i}{t_i}$ as a function of time (τ) for a particular search strategy.

The average time to find the correspondence is then given by

$$\overline{\tau} = \int_0^T \tau\, p(\tau)\, d\tau$$

This integral will be a minimum if the files are ordered so that the blocks are monotonically decreasing along the axis, as shown in Figure 8. 7b, and therefore the secretary should arrange the search (and thus number the files) in decreasing order of $\dfrac{P_i}{t_i}$. If we compute the value of $\overline{\tau}$ on the basis that the files are so ordered in sequence, then

$$\overline{\tau} = (\frac{P_1}{t_1})(\frac{t_1}{2}) + (\frac{P_2}{t_2})(t_1 + \frac{t_2}{2}) + (\frac{P_3}{t_3})(t_1 + t_2 + \frac{t_3}{2}) + \ldots$$

$$= \frac{P_1}{2} + \frac{P_2}{2} + \ldots + \frac{P_N}{2} + (\frac{P_2}{t_2})(t_1) + (\frac{P_3}{t_3})(t_1 + t_2) + (\frac{P_4}{t_4})(t_1 + t_2 + t_3) + \ldots$$

$$= \frac{1}{2} + (\frac{P_2}{t_2})(t_1) + (\frac{P_3}{t_3})(t_1 + t_2) + (\frac{P_4}{t_4})(t_1 + t_2 + t_3) + \ldots + (\frac{P_N}{t_N})(t_1 + \ldots + t_{N-1})$$

where $\dfrac{P_1}{t_1} \leq \dfrac{P_2}{t_2} \leq \dfrac{P_3}{t_3} \leq \dfrac{P_4}{t_4} \ldots \leq \dfrac{P_N}{t_N}$.

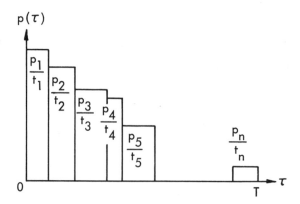

Figure 8. 7b. The quantity $\dfrac{P_i}{t_i}$ as a function of time (τ) for the search strategy which minimizes $\bar{\tau}$.

From the last expression it is clear that the interchanging of the order of any two files in the sequence will increase the value of $\bar{\tau}$. To prove this, one has only to interchange the two values and subtract this new value of $\bar{\tau}$ from the old one and observe that the result is positive.

Example 8. 3. In a local Western Union telegraph office which employs only one delivery boy, it is noticed that there is frequently a large backlog of telegrams to be delivered. It is estimated that the arrival of telegrams follows a Poisson distribution with mean λ, and the time for delivery of one telegram is exponentially distributed with mean $\dfrac{1}{\mu}$. Two suggestions are made that would alleviate the situation: (1) Hire a second delivery boy so that two telegrams may be delivered simultaneously. (2) Double the average delivery rate (This might be done by trading in the delivery bicycle for a motor scooter). Which plan would minimize the number of telegrams waiting to be delivered? Would that also minimize the average number of telegrams in the system?

To solve any problem it is always necessary to make some assumptions which will permit us to develop a mathematical model which simulates the operation. We shall assume that in all cases a delivery boy takes from the office only one telegram at a time and delivers it, whereupon he returns to the office and, if another one is in the basket, he picks it up and delivers that one. This is equivalent, of course, to the assumption that very few of the telegrams are to be delivered to the same neigh-

borhood during a short interval of time. We also shall assume
(as indicated above) that the telegrams arrive at the Western
Union office individually and collectively at random so that the
interarrival time is exponential. Also, the time that it takes
from the moment the boy picks up the telegram until he arrives
back at the office is also exponentially distributed.

It must be remembered that, according to the Poisson assumption, only one event can take place during an interval of time dt.
As in all problems involving distribution functions, it is necessary to define all of the possible states of the system. We shall
define our states as 0, 1, 2, etc., indicating, respectively, that
there are no telegrams in the system, one telegram in the system, two telegrams in the system, etc., and define the corresponding probabilities as P_0, P_1, P_2. A telegram is in the
system if it is either in the basket at the Western Union office
or is being delivered by a boy. Under these assumptions, what
are the answers to the questions?

Case I. Let us consider the first case of two boys, each
with a bicycle and each with an average service time to deliver
a telegram of $\frac{1}{\mu}$. Let n be the number of telegrams in the
system including those in the boys' hands. We are now able to
develop a system of equations which relate the change in the
probability of being in a particular state with time. One must
remember that only one event is possible in the interval of
time dt, and therefore we do not have to take into consideration
the joint occurrence of several events. Most important, however, is the fact that the probabilities can be computed independently of any past history. The plus sign on the right-hand side
of the equations indicates when the probability is increased by
the occurrence of an event, and the negative when it is decreased.

$$dP_0 = (\mu\, dt)P_1 - (\lambda dt)P_0$$

$$dP_1 = (2\mu dt)P_2 + (\lambda dt)P_0 - (\mu dt)P_1 - (\lambda dt)P_1$$

$$dP_2 = (2\mu dt)P_3 + (\lambda dt)P_1 - (2\mu dt)P_2 - (\lambda dt)P_2$$

$$dP_3 = (2\mu dt)P_4 + (\lambda dt)P_2 - (2\mu dt)P_3 - (\lambda dt)P_3$$

The first equation says that the change in the probability of
being in state zero is contributed to positively by being in the
state 1 and completing the delivery of a telegram in the interval
of time dt. This event has a probability of occurrence of μdt
by the Poisson assumption. We can get out of this state
(negative) by having no telegram in the system at time t and
having one arrive during dt.

The second equation indicates that the change in the probability of being in state 1 is affected by four possibilities: being in state 2 and having a delivery accomplished during dt (note $2\mu dt$ here, since two boys); being in state zero and having an arrival (probability μdt); being in state 1 and having either an arrival or completing a delivery (probability μdt or λdt), which terms are negative since we get out of the state 1 by their occurrence. Similar arguments hold for all the other possible states.

If we are interested only in the steady-state probabilities, each derivative, $\dfrac{dP_0}{dt}$, $\dfrac{dP_1}{dt}$, etc., can be set equal to zero; this reduces our set of differential equations to an infinite set of linear equations for the probabilities P_0, P_1, P_2, ... These can be solved recursively with the added restriction that

$$\sum_{n=0}^{\infty} P_n = 1,$$

yielding

$$P_n = 2\rho^n \left(\frac{1 - \rho}{1 + \rho}\right) \text{ for } n \geq 1,$$

where $\rho = \dfrac{\lambda}{2\mu}$ and $n = 0, 1, 2, 3, \ldots$. The expected number in the system is, by definition

$$E(n) - \sum_{0}^{\infty} n P_n = \frac{2\rho}{1 - \rho^2} \text{ if } \rho < 1$$

and the expected number waiting to be delivered is

$$E(n - 2) = \sum_{2}^{\infty} (n - 2) P(n) = \frac{2\rho^3}{1 - \rho^2}$$

Case II. Now consider one boy with a motor scooter and thus an exponential service time of $\dfrac{1}{2\mu}$. The equations then become

$$dP_0 = (2\mu dt)P_1 - (\lambda dt)P_0$$

$$dP_1 = (2\mu dt)P_2 + (\lambda dt)P_0 - (2\mu dt)P_1 - (\lambda dt)P_1$$

$$dP_2 = (2\mu dt)P_3 + (\lambda dt)P_1 - (2\mu dt)P_2 - (\lambda dt)P_2$$

$$\vdots \qquad \vdots \qquad \vdots \qquad \vdots$$

Solving this infinite set for the steady-state conditions, we arrive at the probabilities as:

$$P_n = \rho^n(1 - \rho) \text{ for } \rho < 1,$$

where $P = \dfrac{\lambda}{2\mu}$ and $n = 0, 1, 2, \ldots$. Thus, the expected number in the system is

$$E(n) = \sum_0^\infty \mu\, P_n = \frac{\rho}{1 - \rho}$$

and, correspondingly, the expected number waiting is

$$E(n - 1) = \sum_1^\infty (n - 1)\rho^n(1 - \rho) = \frac{\rho^2}{1 - \rho}$$

Since

$$\frac{\rho}{1 - \rho} < \frac{2\rho}{1 - \rho^2}$$

for $\rho < 1$, one boy with a motor scooter minimizes the average number of telegrams in the system.

But since

$$\frac{2\rho^3}{1 - \rho^2} < \frac{\rho^2}{1 - \rho}$$

for $\rho < 1$, two boys minimize the number of telegrams at the office waiting for delivery.

It should be emphasized that this illustrates a very important fact, namely, that the best strategy depends upon the measure of effectiveness decided upon or on what one wishes to accomplish by the operation.

References

1. Morse, P. M., Queues, Inventories and Maintenance, John Wiley & Sons, Inc., New York, 1958.

2. Notes on Operations Research 1959, Operations Research Center, M. I. T., The Technology Press, Massachusetts Institute of Technology, Cambridge, Mass., 1959.

3. Wadsworth, G. P., and J. G. Bryan, Introduction to Probability and Random Variables, McGraw-Hill Book Co., Inc., New York, 1960.

Chapter 9

MATHEMATICAL TECHNIQUES:
MATHEMATICAL PROGRAMMING

John D. C. Little

This Chapter describes briefly what mathematical programming is, the classes of problems it tries to solve, and several applications in public systems.

9.1 General Remarks

Mathematical programming is concerned with the maximization (or minimization) of a function of many variables, particularly in the case where the values of the variables are restricted in some way. Thus, given a numerically measurable objective and given mathematical relations that specify how various available actions relate to each other and to the objective, we seek to determine "how much of what to do when" in order to achieve the largest value of the stated objective. This is an optimization, or <u>mathematical programming</u>, problem.

The term "programming" comes from "program" in the sense of a schedule of activities. The first use of the term was in "linear programming," which evolved after the close of World War II from research on the planning of military activities. Many problems outside of planning involve optimization. Due to the success of linear programming, the word "programming" has been generalized to a rather broad mathematical field.

In a world where improvement is constantly sought, one might expect that optimization would be a big subject and, indeed, it is. There are dozens of books and hundreds of papers on mathematical programming. One can safely assume that at this moment some computer is working on the numerical solution of a practical problem. Two contemporary circumstances have given great impetus to the field. One is the increasing complexity of the problems we want to solve; many important problems involve large numbers of interrelated variables. The other is the rise of the computer; this has made it possible to solve large problems. Virtually all mathematical programming methods are developed with the computer in mind. The output of the theory is seldom an explicit formula, like

$A = \pi r^2$. Almost always the output is an algorithm, or numerical procedure, like that used in doing long division, where a
rigid set of operations is performed over and over on a set of
input data until eventually an appropriate numerical answer is
produced.

Strictly speaking, mathematical programming as a field
starts after a problem has been formulated in mathematical
terms. One might conjecture, therefore, that practical prob-
lem-solving could be done in two stages: (1) model formulation and (2) model solution. This works only up to a point.
The world is more malleable than we might think -- or at least
our representations of it are. Small changes in a model may
have little operational significance but great computational significance. It is a truism, but cooperation is needed between
the man who formulates the problem and the man who solves
it, if, indeed, they are not the same person.

Most of our space below will be devoted to linear programming. Other topics are described by contrast. We shall
thereby introduce the principal dichotomies of the field: linear
vs. nonlinear programming; continuous vs. integer variables;
deterministic vs. stochastic problems.

9.2 Linear Programming

Linear programming deals with maximization (or minimization) of a linear expression whose variables are subject to
constraints in the form of linear equalities or inequalities.

Thus, in a forestry management problem, suppose we wish
to find numerical values for the variables:

x_1 = acres planted in time period 1
x_2 = acres planted in time period 2
x_3 = acres improved by thinning in period 1
x_4 = acres improved by thinning in period 2
x_5 = acres cut in period 1
x_6 = acres cut in period 2
$\vdots$
x_n = acres left untouched.

Suppose further that five cost units are required to plant an
acre in time period 1, six cost units in time period 2, three
cost units to thin an acre in period 1, etc. Letting z denote
total cost, we have

$$\text{total cost} = z = 5x_1 + 6x_2 + 3x_3 + \ldots + 0x_n$$

We wish to minimize cost. One good idea seems to be to set

all the x's to zero. Then there would be no cost. Better yet,
set some of the variables negative and make a profit. Clearly,
negative values are nonsense. We therefore adopt the constraints $x_i \geq 0$ for all i. To have all the variables zero is
presumably nonsense too. For example, there may be a con-
straint that the total acreage to be cut must be at least some
specified amount to meet contractual obligations. Perhaps

$$x_5 + x_6 \geq 7,000$$

In addition, it may be required that new planting equals cutting:

$$x_1 + x_2 = x_5 + x_6$$

In such a manner we develop a set of constraints on the x's.
The constraints, provided they are linear, along with the
linear cost function comprise a linear program.

Any linear programming problem can always be put in the
following form:
 LP1: Find values for $x_1, x_2, \ldots, x_n$ to minimize

$$z = c_1 x_1 + c_2 x_2 + \ldots + c_n x_n$$

subject to the constraints

$$a_{11} x_1 + \ldots + a_{1n} x_n = b_1$$
$$\vdots$$
$$a_{m1} x_1 + \ldots + a_{mn} x_n = b_m$$
$$x_1, x_2, \ldots, x_n \geq 0$$

Here the a's, b's, and c's are known constants given in the
problem formulation. A problem in inequalities can always be
converted by mathematical devices to one in equalities and a
maximization can be converted to minimization by changing the
algebraic sign of the objective function.

LP1 can be solved by the simplex algorithm, an orderly,
efficient, numerical procedure. Usually, the first task is to
find a set of x's that is feasible, that is, satisfy the constraints
of the problem; then the second task is to go on to find a set
that is optimal. Sometimes, no feasible solution may exist,
although this is often evidence of incorrect problem formulation. Problems involving 1,000 variables and 500 constraining
equations are not uncommon and may be solved without great
difficulty on a large computer.

A curious and useful mathematical property of a linear program is the following: To every linear program there corres-

ponds another linear program, called the <u>dual</u>, made up of new variables but the same constants, now arranged in a new form. The dual of LP1 is:

    <u>LP2:</u> Find values for y_1, y_2, ..., y_m to maximize

$$w = b_1 y_1 + b_2 y_2 + \ldots + b_m y_m$$

subject to the constraints

$$a_{11} y_1 + \ldots + a_m \ y_m \geq c_1$$
$$\vdots \qquad\qquad\qquad \vdots$$
$$a_{1n} y_1 + \ldots + a_{mn} y_m \geq c_n$$

$$y_1, y_2, \ldots, y_m \quad \text{unrestricted in sign}$$

One remarkable property of the two LP's is that, if both have feasible solutions, then min z = max w, i.e., the optimal values of the objective functions are the same. An important practical property is that, if in LP1 we make a small change in a constant b_i, the resulting change in the optimal objective function, z, can be computed from:

$$(\text{Change in } z) = (y_i)(\text{change in } b_i)$$

where y_i comes from the solution of the dual. Thus if b_i is, say, the capacity of a machine, we are computing how much the total cost would be changed if we increased that capacity. In this manner the dual solution sometimes suggests ways to improve the system itself, as opposed to just telling how to operate it at minimum cost.

Computer codes for solving linear programs almost invariably provide the solution to the dual program as well.

<u>9.3 Nonlinear Programming</u>

Some optimization problems cannot be reasonably approximated by linear functions. The general nonlinear programming problem may be written

    <u>NLP:</u> Find values for $x_1, \ldots, x_n$ to maximize

$$z = f(x_1, \ldots, x_n)$$

subject to

$$g_1(x_1, \ldots, x_n) \leq b_1$$
$$\vdots \qquad\qquad\qquad \vdots$$
$$g_m(x_1, \ldots, x_n) \leq b_m$$

where f and the g's are potentially nonlinear functions of the x's.

It is difficult to specify an efficient procedure for solving the general nonlinear programming problem. Some special cases, however, are in fairly good shape. If f is a quadratic function of a particular type and the g's are linear, an efficient algorithm is available. If f and the g's can each be expressed as the sum of functions each of which involves only one of the x's, the problem is called separable, and special methods are available for treating it. Nonlinear functions are often approximated by piece-wise linear functions, and then algorithms are devised that use linear programming, or at least simplex steps. Perhaps the greatest difficulty with nonlinear problems is the possibility of local optima. Thus, in the one-variable case, the objective function might look like Figure 9.1

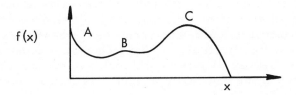

Figure 9.1. Multiple maxima.

Many optimization methods are myopic, and in trying to maximize f(x) one might end up at A or B instead of C. However, sometimes the person setting up the problem knows enough about it to avoid these difficulties.

9.4 Integer Programming

If the x's in LP1 are required to be integers, we have an integer linear program. If some but not all are so restricted, we have a mixed-integer problem. Integer variables are a frequent complication and a serious one. Gomory (see Dantzig[4]) has devised algorithms for these cases and has shown that the algorithms must converge in a finite number of steps. Unfortunately, however, there are some very large finite numbers, and convergence in a reasonable time does not always occur. From a practical point of view, problems with a few integer variables (say, twenty) can usually be solved by one or another of the currently available methods. One approach that has sometimes been helpful is to use branch and bound methods. For a discussion of these, see Lawler and Wood.[7]

9.5 Stochastic Programming

Part of a problem may well involve chance elements or random variables. Sometimes only average values are important
and the problem may be linear in these. Then a straightforward
linear program results. However, the situation is often more
complicated. For example, the probability of some undesirable
outcome may enter as an objective (minimize risk) or as a con-
straint (maximize return, subject to risk being less than or
equal to some value). Since random elements can enter a problem in many ways, a variety of stochastic programming problems
can be defined. Some of them are discussed in Hadley,[5] Chapter
5.

9.6 Dynamic Programming

"Dynamic programming" refers more to a computational
technique than to a class of problems. The technique is quite
powerful in some cases although of little value in others.
Dynamic programming was conceived in response to problems
of optimization in multi-stage processes where the stages were
all mathematically similar. The technique is most useful in
problems that can be viewed in a multi-stage manner whether
or not they arose physically in such a situation. Hadley[5] discusses the technique.

9.7 Heuristic Programming

When formal optimizing algorithms do not exist or are inefficient, there may still be some sensible things to do. One
approach is to imitate the processes that human beings might
use in trying to solve a problem, for example, to use selective
cut-and-try methods, rules of thumb, and devices for capital-
izing on special properties of the problem class. Such procedures are usually called heuristics and often provide good but
not necessarily optimal solutions.

In the same spirit various formal search methods have been
developed. These include one-variable-at-a-time search,
steepest-ascent methods, and random search. Each has been
used with some degree of success and none appears to be a
universal solvent. A useful strategy is to make available a
variety of computer programs to try out on a new problem.

9.8 Applications in Public Systems

The number of applications of mathematical programming to
public, non-military problems is growing rather rapidly. Without trying to be exhaustive or even representative, and without
endorsing the particular approaches used, we report a number

of areas of application that have recently appeared in the operations research literature.

Transportation. This has been a fruitful area for mathematical programming. Elsewhere in this book P. S. Loubal discusses the evaluation of alternative transportation networks. Other examples include the synchronizing of traffic lights[8] and the inferring of traffic distribution on street networks.[2]

Forest Management. A mathematical programming problem here is the determination of cutting and planting schedules to maximize return over a multi-year horizon subject to constraints such as maximum cutting rates, recreational uses of the land, and water runoff limitations.[1,10]

Hospital Menus. Balintfy has been concerned with devising minimum-cost menus subject to diet and variety constraints.

Coupon Schedules for Municipal Bonds. Cohen and Hammer[3] consider the problem of minimizing the net interest cost to a municipality subject to selling the bonds and meeting various institutional constraints.

Water Resource Use. A variety of planning and scheduling problems can be defined in this area. For example, it may be desired to use stream flow and stored water to maximize benefits in the form of energy and irrigated land subject to requirements on firm power and minimum irrigated acreage.[9]

Political Districting. The Supreme Court's one-man-one-vote decision has brought about a great deal of redistricting in the states. Hess, et al.[6] present mathematical programming methods for non-partisan redistricting by computer.

In summary, mathematical programming is an active, growing field with a variety of existing and potential applications in the public domain.

References

1. Broido, A., R. J. McConner, and W. G. O'Regan, "Some Operations Research Applications in the Conservation of Wildland Resources," Management Science (Series A), 11, 802 (July, 1965).

2. Charnes, A., and W. W. Cooper, "Multicopy Traffic Network Models," in R. Herman, ed., Theory of Traffic Flow, Elsevier, Amsterdam, 1961.

3. Cohen, K. J., and F. S. Hammer, "Optimal Coupon Schedules for Municipal Bonds," Management Science (Series A), 12, 68 (September, 1965).

4. Dantzig, G. B., Linear Programming and Extensions, Princeton University Press, Princeton, N. J., 1963.

5. Hadley, G. , <u>Nonlinear and Dynamic Programming,</u> Addison-
    Wesley Publishing Co. , Inc. , Reading, Mass. , 1964.

6. Hess, S. W. , J. B. Weaver, H. J. Seigfeldt, J. N. Whelan,
    and P. A. Zitlan, "Nonpartisan Political Redistricting by
    Computer," <u>Operations Research,</u> 13, 998 (November,
    1965).

7. Lawler, E. L. , and D. E. Wood, "Branch and Bound
    Methods: A Survey," <u>Operations Research,</u> 14, 699
    (July, 1966).

8. Little, J. D. C. , "The Synchronization of Traffic Signals by
    Mixed-Integer Linear Programming," <u>Operations Re-
    search,</u> 14, 568 (July, 1966).

9. Thomas, H. A. , Jr. , and R. Revelle, "On the Efficient
    Use of High Aswan Dam for Hydropower and Irrigation,"
    <u>Management Science (Series B),</u> 12, B-296 (April, 1966).

10. Wardle, P. A. , "Forest Management and Operational
    Research: A Linear Programming Study," <u>Management
    Science (Series B),</u> 11, B-260 (August, 1965).

LIST OF LECTURERS

Special Summer Program
"Operations Research in Public Affairs"
September 6-10, 1966, M. I. T.

ALFRED BLUMSTEIN

Director of Science and Technology
Task Force of President's Commission on
  Law Enforcement and Administration of Justice
Institute for Defense Analyses
Arlington, Virginia

W. E. CUSHEN

Director of Program Analysis and
  Chief of Technical Analysis Division
Institute for Applied Technology
National Bureau of Standards
Washington, D. C.

ALVIN W. DRAKE

Associate Director, Operations Research Center
  and Associate Professor of Electrical Engineering
Massachusetts Institute of Technology
Cambridge, Massachusetts

LESLIE C. EDIE

Engineer of Operations Research
The Port of New York Authority
New York, New York

MARTIN L. ERNST

Vice President, Operations Research Division
Arthur D. Little, Inc.
Cambridge, Massachusetts

WILLIAM J. HORVATH

Assistant Director, Mental Health Research Institute
The University of Michigan
Ann Arbor, Michigan

JOHN D. C. LITTLE

Professor of Management
Massachusetts Institute of Technology
Cambridge, Massachusetts

PETER S. LOUBAL

Head, Transportation Models Group
Bay Area Transportation Study
Berkeley, California

PHILIP M. MORSE

Director, Operations Research Center
Massachusetts Institute of Technology
Cambridge, Massachusetts

DAVID SMITH

Associate Director of Administration
The New York Blood Center
New York, New York

GEORGE P. WADSWORTH

Professor of Mathematics
Massachusetts Institute of Technology
Cambridge, Massachusetts

R. A. WARD

Director, Local Government Operational Research Unit
Reading, U. K.

HARRY B. WOLFE

Manager, Operations Research Section
Western Division
Arthur D. Little, Inc.
San Francisco, California

INDEX